Elite • 175

World War II US Cavalry Units

Pacific Theater

GORDON L ROTTMAN

ILLUSTRATED BY PETER DENNIS

Consultant editor Martin Windrow

First published in Great Britain in 2009 by Osprey Publishing,
Midland House, West Way, Botley, Oxford OX2 0PH, UK
443 Park Avenue South, New York, NY 10016, USA
Email: info@ospreypublishing.com

Print ISBN: 978 184603 451 0
ebook ISBN: 978 1 84908 116 0

Editor: Martin Windrow
Design: Ken Vail Graphic Design, Cambridge, UK (kvgd.com)
Typeset in Sabon and Myriad Pro
Index by Sandra Shotter
Originated by PDQ Digital Media Solutions, UK
Printed in China through World Print Ltd.

09 10 11 12 13 14 9 8 7 6 5 4 3 2 1

A CIP catalog record for this book is available from the British Library

FOR A CATALOGUE OF ALL BOOKS PUBLISHED BY OSPREY MILITARY
AND AVIATION PLEASE CONTACT:

Osprey Direct, c/o Random House Distribution Center,
400 Hahn Road, Westminster, MD 21157
Email: uscustomerservice@ospreypublishing.com

Osprey Direct, The Book Service Ltd, Distribution Centre,
Colchester Road, Frating Green, Colchester, Essex, CO7 7DW
E-mail: customerservice@ospreypublishing.com

www.ospreypublishing.com

ARTIST'S NOTE

THE WOODLAND TRUST

Osprey Publishing are supporting the Woodland Trust, the UK's leading
woodland conservation charity, by funding the dedication of trees.

CONTENTS

WORLD WAR II US CAVALRY UNITS

INTRODUCTION

Historically, armies are reduced after the end of major wars, but nevertheless the regular US Cavalry was expanded following the Civil War from six to ten regiments. During the opening of the West all ten units were scattered across the vast tracts of country west of the Mississippi. By the late 1880s, with the subjugation of the Native American peoples almost complete, over 90 companies/troops were distributed between 31 posts in the West, averaging two companies/troops per post though with up to four in some cases. While the virtual end of active campaigning did not see the number of regiments reduced, each did lose two companies/troops. The 1898 Spanish-American War saw no increase in the regular cavalry, although a few militia and volunteer units also served. In Cuba the 1st, 3d, 6th, 9th, and 10th Cavalry and the 1st US Volunteer Cavalry ("Rough Riders") all fought dismounted as infantry. Thereafter the ongoing insurgency in the Philippines led to the authorization in 1901 of the 11th through 15th Cavalry; these too mostly fought dismounted.

The 16th and 17th Cavalry were activated in 1916. Some regular cavalry regiments served on the Mexican border (as did smaller National Guard units, created from the state militias by the Militia Act of 1903), where their horse-mounted mobility proved valuable. America's entry into World War I saw the activation of the 18th through 25th Cavalry, but all were immediately converted to artillery, as were the Federalized National Guard cavalry units – cavalry was unnecessary on the Western Front, and it made sense to convert them to horse-drawn artillery. Four regular regiments accompanied the American Expeditionary Force to France, where they provided remount services. At the end of 1917 the 15th Cavalry Division was organized at Ft Bliss, Texas, to have three three-regiment brigades, but only the 1st, 7th, 8th, and 10th Cavalry were actually assigned before the division was inactivated in May 1918.

A technician 4th grade, wearing khakis and M1931 lace-up cavalry boots, mounted on the M1928 McClellan saddle. Note the rarely-seen special leather saddle-scabbard for the .30cal M1 carbine. (US Army)

THE INTERWAR YEARS

The introduction of tanks to the battlefield during World War I, coupled with increasing mechanization, the lethality of modern weapons, and the drastically changing nature of maneuver warfare all heralded the beginning of the end for the horse cavalry. The US Cavalry was slow to adopt mechanization, and proponents of horse cavalry sometimes contrived unlikely scenarios in order to justify their retention.

In 1920 two cavalry divisions were authorized, the 1st to be active and the 2d inactive. The division had two two-regiment brigades plus brigade machine-gun squadrons. The 1st Cavalry Division's assigned regiments were the 1st, 7th, 8th, and 10th, the last being replaced by the 5th in 1922. The division also had a single artillery battalion, an engineer battalion, division trains and HQ, signal, ordnance maintenance, medical, and veterinary companies. In 1933 the 12th Cavalry replaced the 1st Cavalry. The 2d Cavalry Division did not have an active headquarters until April 1940. A "paper" 3d Cavalry Division existed during 1927–40, with the 6th (1927–39), 9th (1933–39), 10th (1927–40) and 11th Cavalry (1927–33); it had no headquarters, and its units were merely administrative assignments. Three cavalry regiments, 15th to 17th, were inactivated in 1921, but the 26th Cavalry (Philippine Scouts) was activated on Luzon in 1922. The remaining regiments were each reduced to two three-troop squadrons along with HQ and service troops, and the machine-gun troop was eliminated. In 1928 the squadrons each lost a troop, but the regimental machine-gun troop was reestablished, with the loss of the brigade machine-gun squadron. Trucks began to replace horse-drawn wagons.

The basic cavalry unit was the eight-man rifle squad. Well into the war it retained an organization of a corporal squad leader, second-in-command, two scouts and four riflemen, all privates and privates first class; two of the riflemen remained in the saddle as horse-holders when the other six dismounted. (US Army)

1st Cavalry Division troopers ride across an open area in a dispersed formation during the August 1940 Louisiana Maneuvers. The Cavalry made a bold effort to demonstrate that it was still viable in modern warfare, but it soon became apparent that horse cavalry, while having its uses, was outmaneuvered by mechanized units. (1st Cavalry Division Museum)

In 1928 the development of armored and mechanized forces in the US Army began in earnest. Some cavalrymen accepted the eventual demise of horse cavalry, but others resisted. The Chief of Cavalry, MajGen John Herr, believed that a mix of horse and mechanized forces was necessary: "We must not be misled to our own detriment to assume that the untried machine can displace the proved and tried horse." The Army Chief of Staff, Gen Douglas MacArthur, foretold the future of the cavalry: "The horse has no higher degree of mobility today than he had a thousand years ago. The time has therefore arrived when the Cavalry arm must either replace or assist the horse as a means of transportation, or else pass into the limbo of discarded military formations. There is no possibility of eliminating the need for certain units capable of performing more distant missions than can be efficiently carried out by the mass of the Army. The elements assigned to these tasks will be the cavalry of the future, but manifestly the horse alone will not meet its requirements in transportation."

A THE CAVALRYMAN AND HIS MOUNT, c.1940

Horses required a great deal of care and much of a cavalryman's time was dedicated to this end. There was an old cavalry adage, "Take care of your horse first, and if there is nothing else to do, take care of yourself." After a day's or even half a day's mounted training it required one or two hours to care for the mounts – that is, in addition to the routine daily chores of feeding, watering, exercising when not taken out for riding, grooming, and mucking out the stalls. Then there were the related details of general stables cleaning, moving and storing forage and feed, cleaning and maintaining the considerable tack (horse equipment), and occasional horseshoeing and veterinary treatment. Not only were the troopers and their equipment and quarters closely inspected on Saturdays, but the horses, tack, and stables were too, which demanded even more time than the troopers spent on their own upkeep.

The trooper wears the pre-war blue denim fatigue uniform and hat. The M1912 horse cover protected mounts in cold weather and prevented them from cooling down too fast. Grooming tools included the handheld horse clipper, M1912 horse brush, and curry comb, the latter used to clean off caked dust or mud. Other gear used in the field included the M1941 galvanized feed tub, canvas 4½-gal bucket, and a stand-mounted, hand-powered horse clipper. The M1918 canvas watering trough was portable; it could be rolled up and then erected with six steel stakes driven in wherever needed. Rather than the usual bridle headstall this horse is fitted with a cavesson used for exercising and training horses.

(Inset) The 1st Cavalry Division patch was among the largest in the Army and was referred to as "the saddle blanket."

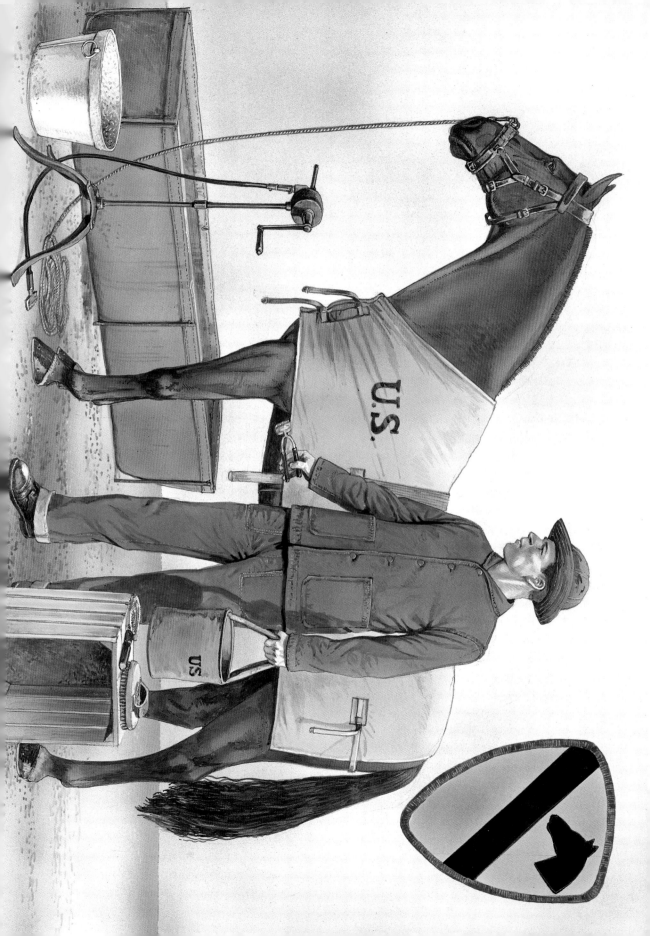

1st Cavalry Division machine-gun troop gunners practice firing the .30cal Browning M1917A1. These water-cooled guns were retained in the dismounted squadrons' weapons troops. (1st Cavalry Division Museum)

Five missions were envisioned for horse cavalry regiments: (1) reconnaissance for large formations; (2) offensive maneuver over broken terrain impassable to tanks and trucks; (3) to relieve an infantry regiment in a quiet sector allowing the infantry to engage elsewhere – economy-of-force; (4) as a covering force forward of the main line of resistance, to delay an advancing enemy and confuse him on the location of the MLR; (5) to move rapidly to block a breach in the MLR.

Both the cavalry and infantry became involved in the development of tanks and a doctrine for their employment. The 1st and 13th Cavalry were converted to mechanized units with combat cars (light tanks) and scout cars, the 4th and 6th to mechanized horse regiments with truck-drawn vans to transport horses long distances, and the other 11 remained horse regiments.[1] There were 18 National Guard regiments in the 21st through 24th Cavalry Divisions, and 24 in the Reserve's 61st through 66th Cavalry Divisions; these were skeleton units.

PRE-WAR CAVALRY REGIMENTS

The National Guard's four cavalry divisions were inactivated in late 1940 when the Army judged them unnecessary for war plans. Most of the regiments were converted to mechanized cavalry groups or cavalry reconnaissance squadrons in late 1943 and early 1944, and others to artillery units.[2] (The six Reserve cavalry divisions constituted in early 1921 were ordered inactivated in January 1942, and all were by April. None had been

1 Mechanized horse regiments had semi-trailer trucks towing 6-ton combination animal and cargo trailers carrying eight men and eight horses plus their rifles and equipment – a squad.
2 Cavalry groups carried cavalry regiment lineages and were HQs for, typically, two attached cavalry reconnaissance squadrons. These units were equipped with armored cars, light tanks, and halftracks, and were assigned to corps for reconnaissance, screening, covering force, and pursuit missions.

called to active duty, and their units were converted mainly to artillery. The Office of the Chief of Cavalry was closed in March 1942.)

The 2d Cavalry Division was assigned the 2d, 9th, 10th, and 14th Cavalry, while the 3d and 11th remained non-divisional horse regiments. The 2d Cavalry Division was active from April 1941 to July 1942. The 1st and 13th Cavalry were converted to armored regiments in 1940 and assigned to armored divisions, as were the 2d, 3d, 11th, and 14th Cavalry in 1942. In February 1943 the 2d Cavalry Division was reactivated with the 9th, 10th, 27th, and 28th Cavalry, all Colored units; sent to North Africa in early 1944, it was inactivated there in May, its personnel being reorganized into engineer and service units.

The only remaining horse cavalry units were the 112th and 124th Cavalry of the Texas National Guard, assigned to the 56th Cavalry Brigade. The 112th would depart for the South Pacific in July 1942, and the 124th for India in July 1944.

THE CONFUSIONS OF DESIGNATION: REGIMENTS, SQUADRONS, COMPANIES AND TROOPS

In Europe a cavalry regiment was generally a battalion-sized unit typically with four to six company-sized "squadrons" made up of platoon-sized "troops." In US service the regiment, commanded by a full colonel, was of the same echelon as an infantry regiment, but the numbers of sub-units actually assigned or authorized to be manned varied over the years. Full-strength regiments were typically authorized ten or 12 companies; the term "troop" was occasionally used to identify companies, but "company"

Wearing winter garb, a cavalryman operates a .30cal Browning M1919A2 cavalry light machine gun, a slightly more compact version of the infantry's M1919A4, identifiable by its slotted barrel jacket. The A4 would replace the A2, but the latter continued to serve alongside it in 1st Cavalry Division units. (1st Cavalry Division Museum)

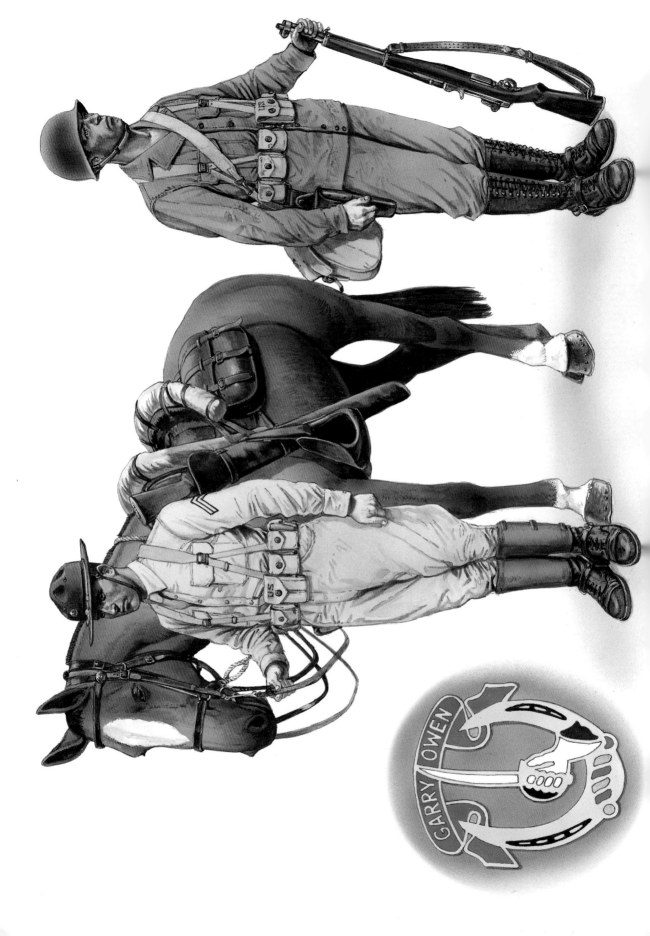

was the more common designation for these units of between 40 and 100 men commanded by captains. After the Civil War the regiment was standardized with 12 companies, although peacetime regiments might have as few as four. "Battalions" and "squadrons" were not standing units but temporary groupings of companies. Some regiments during the Civil War formed squadrons of two companies, commanded by the more senior company commander, and two to three battalions each of two squadrons, commanded by a major. Others used the terms battalion and squadron interchangeably for a grouping of between two and four companies.

From 1873 only the term "troop" was used in documents, but "company" remained in common use; even after 1883, when "troop" was the term specifically directed, "company" remained in use until around the turn of the century. Some regiments even mixed both terms. Eventually "troop" and "squadron" were the only terms used for the company- and battalion-equivalent cavalry units.

European cavalry regiments with four to six troop-sized squadrons clung to the heavy cavalry concept of lances and sabers lending their shock effect to the mass two-rank charge. Between 1911 and 1916 US cavalry regiments similarly consolidated their 12 troops into six larger troops and eliminated the squadron echelon. This was found unsatisfactory because of the frequent need to fight dismounted, and on the Mexican border the one-rank fighting formation was found better suited. The old organization was revived, with three four-troop squadrons, now with additional regimental HQ, supply, and machine-gun troops.

The cavalry division retained the "square" structure of four regiments, with two assigned to each of its two brigades. The 1st Cavalry Division employed cavalry designations for most of its non-cavalry units – e.g., 1st Medical Squadron (comprised of "troops") – rather than battalions and companies. The artillery retained its battalion and battery designations.

B | **THE LAST DAYS OF HORSED CAVALRY: 7th CAVALRY, 1941**

1: On the Texas-Mexico border the cotton khaki uniform was worn much of the year. There was an olive drab wool winter version, and south Texas can be cold from November to February. Cavalrymen wore breeches rather than straight trousers, with M1940 three-strap boots. The M1910 campaign hat, with its distinctive Montana peak, is adorned with a circular badge of the national arms, and gold-yellow Cavalry cords. The corporal's chevrons, in light OD on dark blue, are worn on both sleeves.

2: While the olive drab fatigue uniform was intended to replace the blue denim version in 1941, it was sometimes worn as a field uniform as khakis proved inadequate. The only insignia authorized on fatigues were rank chevrons, but often even these were not worn. Fatigue trousers were to be worn over the cumbersome M1931 lace-up cavalry boots when on stable duty, but worn bloused when riding – an unofficial practice.

Both soldiers' web gear includes M1909 suspenders, M1923 mounted cartridge belt (with nine pockets rather than the ten of the dismounted belt, thus allowing space for the M1923 pistol magazine pocket), M1916 pistol holster with M1911A1 pistol, and M1924 first aid pouch. The canteen was carried on the saddle, but was attached to the belt when dismounted. Even though they used M1 Garand rifles cavalrymen were not issued bayonets. **B2** carries an M1936 musette bag issued to cavalrymen rather than a backpack.

3: The cavalry horse was described as being sound, well bred, of a superior class, having quality, gentle and of kind disposition, and well broken to the saddle. The Army purchased only geldings (neutered) of any darkish color (no grey, white, or too much white – light-colored horses were susceptible to sunburn and skin diseases, and were conspicuous), from five to eight years old , and weighing from 1,000–1,200lb depending on height, which should be 14.2–15.2 hands (one hand = 4in or 10cm). Common breeds were Thoroughbreds, Quarterhorses, Arabians, Morgans, American Saddlers, Standardbreds, Cleveland Bays, Anglo-Arabs, and Morabs.

The roll at the pommel of the saddle is the raincoat, over the folded empty feedbag and grain bag; the roll at the cantle is the blanket and shelter tent section with the tent pole and pins inside. The canteen and cup are attached to the cantle ring and saddlebag on the off side.

(Inset) 7th Cavalry Regiment

HORSE CAVALRY UNIT ORGANIZATION

In the late 1930s the war-strength mounted cavalry regiment was a formidable unit. While this organization did not see combat in World War II except for the 26th Cavalry, its study provides a better understanding of the coming dismounted regiment's structure. The mounted cavalry regiment was organized and armed to deliver a respectable amount of small-arms firepower; its armament was kept light to allow for rapid maneuver, but augmented by significant automatic weapons. There were few mortars, and no antitank guns other than .50cal machine guns (tanks during this period possessed only modest armor). The full war-strength regiment was authorized 78 officers, one warrant officer, 1,608 enlisted men, and 1,812 horses.[3]

There was a regimental HQ troop, service troop, band, and medical detachment. The regiment also possessed a machine-gun troop with three four-gun platoons with .30cal M1917A1s, plus a special weapons platoon with two 60mm M2 mortars and four .50cal M2 heavy MGs; this latter platoon was absorbed into the wartime special weapons troop, which had two four-gun .50cal platoons and a mortar platoon with four 60mm tubes. The HQ troop had a platoon with six Indiana White M1 (T7) scout cars, and numerous trucks were provided to transport service elements.

The 404-man cavalry squadrons, commanded by lieutenant-colonels, had only an eight-man HQ and three rifle troops. A troop commanded by a captain had a 16-man headquarters, a light MG platoon with three squads each armed with one .30cal M1919A2, and three rifle platoons. A rifle platoon had a five-man headquarters and three eight-man squads. Each man in the platoon had an M1 rifle and a pistol, except for the lieutenant with a pistol only. Each officer was authorized a spare horse. No Browning automatic rifles (BAR) were authorized.

Regular regiments might have only two two-troop squadrons, but the Texas NG regiments retained all three squadrons with two troops each until just prior to being Federalized in 1940. The number of horses assigned to peacetime National Guard troops varied over time but they were never at full strength; one example is a troop with three full-time animal caretakers, 26 Federally provided horses, and two accepted (donated) horses.

WARTIME DISMOUNTED CAVALRY ORGANIZATION

Converting a horse cavalry unit to an infantry unit was not simply a matter of turning in horses and saddles and drawing marching boots and backpacks. Cavalry units possessed only modest numbers of supporting crew-served weapons compared to their infantry counterparts, and their strength was much smaller than equivalent-echelon infantry units.

The shortage of crew-served weapons was a significant limitation on the capabilities of dismounted cavalry units. An infantry rifle company possessed

---

3 For comparison, peacetime strength was 41 officers, one warrant officer, 744 enlisted men, and 790 horses. The peacetime regiment lacked a 3d Sqn, there were only two troops per squadron rather than three, and the regimental MG troop was inactive; the regiment thus had roughly the combat power of a battalion.

one BAR per rifle squad to total nine, one 2.36in bazooka per rifle platoon, and two .30cal M1919A4 light machine guns and two 60mm M2 mortars in the weapons platoon. The battalion heavy weapons company had two .30cal M1917A1 heavy machine gun platoons with a total of eight guns, and a platoon of six 81mm mortars. The battalion HQ company possessed three 37mm antitank guns, and a number of bazookas were distributed among the various headquarters elements.

The cavalry troop initially had only a machine-gun platoon with two .30cal and .50cal machine guns each, and the rifle squads lacked BARs. Between 1943 and 1945 a confusing array of directives were issued allocating additional weapons and manning, but there were so many conflicting directives that units could not possibly have followed them to the letter, and there must have been variations in organization and weapon allocations between units. The question is often asked why dismounted units simply did not adopt infantry tables of organization; there is no answer to that, other than a wish to hang onto the vestiges of cavalry organization.

The greatest limitation was the lack of a third squadron. The two National Guard regiments possessed three two-troop squadrons, but were reorganized into two three-troop squadrons when Federalized. This denied the regiment a reserve to reinforce success, relieve an exhausted squadron, block an enemy breakthrough, conduct a counterattack, secure an exposed flank, or perform other tasks.

With augmentation in personnel and equipment, by mid 1944 the 112th Cavalry consisted of a 210-man HQ and HQ troop, a 178-man service troop, a 174-man (infantry battalion-type) weapons troop, a 63-man medical detachment, a 22-man band (serving as litter-bearers in combat – not all regiments had bands), and two 521-man squadrons. The squadrons only had a 20-man HQ and three rifle troops. They were now organized and armed along the same lines as a rifle company, including the addition of a weapons platoon with two light machine guns and two 60mm mortars, and the squads each had a BAR and a Thompson submachine gun. However, there was no squadron-level weapons or HQ troop.

The regimental HQ troop consisted of a troop HQ, communications, intelligence and operations, reconnaissance (12 MG-armed jeeps; the 124th's operated afoot), and antitank (3×37mm) platoons. The service troop had a troop HQ, administrative, motor maintenance, supply transport, train defense (one jeep, four M3 scout cars), and pioneer demolition platoons. The squadron HQ element consisted only of the squadron HQ and a communications platoon. There was no equivalent to the infantry battalion HQ company.

The 1st Cavalry Division's regiments were reorganized along similar lines in December 1943, and the squadrons received infantry battalion-type weapons troops (Troops D and H, or simply Weapons Troop) at the same time; these were also added to the 112th in October 1944. This now gave dismounted regiments both regimental and squadron weapons troops, except in the 124th, which

Cavalry-infantry manpower comparison 1943–44

Cavalry		Infantry	
squad	8	squad	12
platoon	32	platoon	41
troop	165	company	193
squadron	521	battalion	894
regiment	1,726	regiment	3,207

Cavalry branch-of-service brass collar insignia for officers and enlisted men, the latter on an inch-diameter disc.

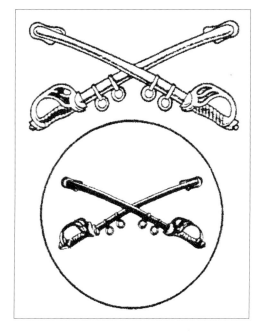

lacked squadron weapons troops. The troop had two platoons each of four .30cal M1917A1 MGs and a platoon of six 81mm M1 mortars. In September 1944 the regimental weapons troop's .30cal MGs were replaced by .50cals, including that in the 124th.

In preparation for the projected invasion of Japan, the 1st Cavalry Division units and 112th Cavalry were finally reorganized as standard infantry regiments in July 1945, but still with only two squadrons and a comparable shortage of regimental support unit elements. The regimental weapons troops were converted to cannon troops with six 105mm M7 self-propelled howitzers, but there was no antitank troop. The squadron and troop designations were retained, as were the two-regiment brigades.

The 124th Cavalry was assigned a 3d Squadron in Burma in September 1944 to give it capabilities similar to its partner 475th Infantry Regiment, though it was still almost a thousand men smaller. It too had a regimental weapons troop, but with just four 81mm mortars (plus an unofficial augmentation of two 4.2-in M2 tubes), but no squadron weapons troops. Its squadron HQs lacked the communications platoon found in other cavalry squadrons.

The comparatively smaller size and lesser capabilities of cavalry regiments limited their potential and disappointed higher commanders in regards to staying power and combat capabilities. After the Arawe operation of winter 1943/44 the 112th Cavalry reported: "The present Cavalry Table of Organization does not provide sufficient firepower for Cavalry acting as Infantry.... While there is considerable difference in the comparative size of Infantry and Cavalry organizations, combat missions and tasks are often assigned on an equal basis." Cavalry units were viewed as mobile rapid-strike units, but dismounted cavalry were no more mobile than infantry and their firepower was much less. With only about half the strength of an infantry regiment they simply could not accomplish the same missions as their infantry counterparts. To alleviate this problem a brigade sometimes attached an extra squadron to one of its regiments to provide three, and the remaining regiment served as a brigade reserve, but often both squadrons of a regiment would be deployed forward with just a single troop retained in regimental reserve. In other situations one brigade retained its two regiments and the other only one, the fourth being retained under division control as a reserve; again, sometimes just a squadron served as the division reserve.

Dismounted cavalry based their tactics on the standard infantry manuals, but they could not absolutely replicate them owing to less manpower and fewer weapons in some categories. The main impact was that units could hold only narrow frontages. This proved unimportant during most operations on Leyte and Luzon; advances followed roads and mountain trails forcing very narrow frontages, with regimental zones often being held by a single forward squadron. However, the cavalry units' smaller strength affected their staying power, since casualties reduced a unit's capabilities quickly.

Machine-gun troop cavalrymen in wool field uniforms preparing to load up their pack horses after an overnight bivouac. Foreground, note the M1911 spurs on M1931 boots. A .30cal M1919A2 machine gun can be seen along with the old-type M1917 wooden ammunition boxes. (1st Cavalry Division Museum)

26th CAVALRY REGIMENT (PHILIPPINE SCOUTS)

Our Strength is in Loyalty

The 26th Cavalry Regiment (PS) was activated on October 1, 1922 at Ft Stotsenburg near Clark Field, some 60 miles north of Manila on central Luzon. Its original troops were drawn from the inactivated 25th Field Artillery and 43d Infantry Regiments of the Philippine Scouts. Raised in 1901, the Scouts were hand-picked volunteer Filipinos led by regular US Army officers and a very small number of Filipino officers who had graduated from West Point. The regiment received a third troop for each of its squadrons in early 1941 and its strength was increased to 52 officers and 784 men. There was also a HQ troop and a machine-gun troop, but no mortars or antitank weapons. The HQ troop did have a platoon with six Indiana White M1 (T7) scout cars, and trucks were provided to transport service elements.

The beginning of the war found the 26th Cavalry under the command of Col Clinton A. Pierce and stationed at Ft Stotsenburg, with Troop F detached to Nichols Field south of Manila. Small Japanese landings occurred on Luzon's north coast on December 10, 1941, but the main landing in Lingayen Gulf northwest of Manila did not take place until December 22. Initial US-Filipino opposition was light but gradually stiffened, even though American airpower had been destroyed. The 26th, supported by elements of the 23d and 24th Field Artillery Regts (PS), made repeated small-scale counterattacks across a broad front to delay the Japanese advance. The regiment lost a quarter of its men and half its horses in the first five days.

An American platoon commander, wearing khakis and the M1917A1 "dishpan" helmet, leads his Philippine Scouts of the 26th Cavalry Regiment across a river. The Philippine Scouts were a component of the US Army and wore the same uniforms and equipment as their American counterparts, but received lower pay and fewer benefits. They were known for their professionalism and discipline, and in 1941 they were career soldiers with an average of 13 years' service – some of them the second generation in their families to have served in the Scouts. (US Army)

The 26th Cavalry was assigned to the North Luzon Force under MajGen Jonathan M. Wainwright along with the 11th, 71st, and 91st Philippine Divisions. The Japanese 48th Div routed the North Luzon Force on December 27, and it began its retreat southward, during which the 26th Cavalry performed scouting, flank screening, and covering force missions. It was especially effective in fighting rearguard actions, greatly aiding the withdrawal by slowing the Japanese pursuit. The regiment performed as dragoons, moving into position on horseback and fighting dismounted before withdrawing by horse. The level terrain of the Agno/Pampanga river valley allowed the horsemen to move quickly from engagement to engagement.

Realizing there was no hope of reinforcement, on December 26 Gen MacArthur ordered the Luzon forces to withdraw to the Bataan peninsula for a last stand. A series of holding and rearguard actions were fought to delay the Japanese, and North Luzon Force hung on to San Fernando to allow South Luzon Force to pass through to Bataan. This was accomplished on January 2, 1942, the same day that the Japanese entered Manila. The last US-Filipino units closed on Bataan on January 6, among them the battered and by now nearly horseless 26th Cavalry. North Luzon Force was reorganized as I Philippine Corps to defend the western portion of the Bataan front, and the 26th Cavalry was ordered to occupy positions on the rugged slopes of Mt Natib, which required hard travel over ravines to reach them on January 9. The Japanese launched their offensive that day. From January 10 to 15 the cavalrymen and their exhausted mounts rested and were re-shoed. The supply situation soon became desperate, with the troopers growing weaker on half-rations and no feed or forage available for the horses, which began dying off – the grazing in the mountain jungle was inadequate. The 26th fought as infantry, dug-in in intricate mountainside defensive positions.

The last cavalry charge in the US Army's history occurred on January 16.[4] Lieutenant Ramsey's Troop F was ordered to secure the village of Morong on the west coast of Bataan. Upon arrival the cavalrymen found hundreds of Japanese troops entering the village from across a river, and the troop commander immediately ordered his lead platoon to charge into them. With the cavalry firing at point-blank ranges many Japanese fled across the river, and Ramsey established a skirmish line to hold them at bay while his two following platoons came up, followed by Filipino infantry (see Plate B).

While US-Filipino forces were pushed south the Japanese suspended the offensive on February 8 for rest and reinforcement. They resumed their attacks on March 12, but it was not until April 3 that the main offensive was launched on the east coast by the 4th Div and 65th Brigade. The 26th Cavalry served as a covering force in the mountainous sector between I and II Corps. With the troops severely weakened by relentless combat, hunger, illness, and the brutal climate, on March 15 it was ordered that the remaining 250 horses and 48 mules be slaughtered; along with curry and rice, the horsemeat provided valuable nourishment for the half-starved Bataan defenders. On April 7 the regiment was attached to II Corps, but it still operated in the center sector of the line. The front finally collapsed under relentless assault, and on April 9, 1942, the Bataan Force surrendered to the Japanese Fourteenth Army. The 26th Cavalry passed into history as the few hundred

4 The last large-scale US cavalry charge was conducted by the 11th Cavalry and attached Apache Scouts against Poncho Villa's irregular cavalry at Rancho Ojos Azules, Mexico, on May 5, 1916.

surviving troopers staggered into captivity; many would die on the Bataan Death March and in the prison camps. Most Filipino prisoners were paroled in July, and large numbers joined the guerrillas.

Parts of Troop C and two 43d Infantry (PS) companies were isolated in northern Luzon and provided the core for guerrilla units; a few other 26th Cavalry officers and Filipino troopers were able to escape and fight on with the guerrillas. The 26th Cavalry was formally disbanded on April 23, 1946 at Ft Stotsenburg and its two squadrons likewise in 1951 – on paper only, since the units were already inactive.

The 26th Cavalry HQ Troop's scout platoon was equipped with six of these Indiana White M1 (formerly T7) scout cars. They were armed with a .50cal M2 and two .30cal M1919A2 machine guns on running-board pedestal mounts. This 1934 vehicle was the predecessor of the better-known White M3A1 scout car, which saw wide use early in the war. (US Army)

TEXAS NATIONAL GUARD CAVALRY: BACKGROUND

After the Civil War, Texas reestablished militia units in 1876; unlike most Southern states it did not pick up the lineages of Civil War units but began new lineages. The 1st Texas Cavalry was one of these; over the years the unit's companies were relocated from town to town, and it never exceeded squadron strength. To replace the Regular Army's 15th Cavalry Division, planned for inactivation in May 1918, Texas was directed to raise two cavalry brigades, but only the 1st Cavalry Brigade, Texas National Guard was activated, in January 1918 in Houston; it consisted of the 2d (San Antonio), 3d (Brenham), 4th (Amarillo), 5th (Dallas), 6th (Texarkana), and 7th (Houston) Texas Cavalry Regiments, the original 1st Texas Cavalry being broken up to form these new "regiments." In 1920, with the post-World War I reestablishment of the Texas NG, the 1st Cav Bde was redesignated 56th Cav Bde on December 14, and at the same time the skeleton regiments were

OUR STRENGTH IS IN LOYALTY

consolidated into a new 1st Texas Cavalry with headquarters in Dallas. On July 20, 1921 the 1st Texas Cavalry was redesignated 112th Cavalry. Other brigade units were the Brigade HQ Troop, 56th Machine Gun Squadron in Houston, and 111th Cavalry of the New Mexico NG (a "paper" unit). In February 1929 the 112th's 2d Sqn and the 56th MG Sqn provided the basis for the new 124th Cavalry as the 1st and 2d Sqns respectively. The 111th, which had never physically served with the brigade, was released. The brigade HQ in Houston became the 124th's HQ Troop and a new brigade HQ was organized in San Antonio. The 3d Sqn was raised in 1939.

Troopers of the Texas National Guard's 112th Cavalry at Ft Bliss, Texas; standing before their stables, they await the order to mount up. They wear olive drab fatigues and carry M1 rifles in their saddle scabbards. (Texas Military Forces Museum)

C THE LAST CAVALRY CHARGE: 26th CAVALRY, JANUARY 1942

The last cavalry charge in the US Army's history occurred on January 16, 1942. The 26th Cavalry (Philippine Scouts) had been on the Bataan peninsula for a week and a half, and US-Filipino forces were still consolidating their positions and attempting to stabilize the front under continuous Japanese assault. The regiment's Troop F, under 1st Lt Edwin P. Ramsey, was ordered to occupy the upper west coast village of Morong before the Japanese reached it. The advancing cavalrymen found hundreds of troops of the 65th Brigade entering the village, with more wading the river on the far side of the *barrio*. Recognizing that the situation could only be reversed by immediate bold action, Lt Ramsey ordered his 27-man lead platoon to charge into the middle of the unsuspecting Japanese. The saber was abolished in 1934; charges were conducted with .45cal pistols, and troopers were also armed with .30cal M1 Garand rifles. Ramsey led the galloping horses and yelling troopers headlong into the small village, firing at point-blank ranges. Few of the panicked Japanese returned fire and most fled across the river, where many were cut down. Ramsey established a skirmish line to hold them at bay while his two following platoons came up. There were still scattered Japanese in Morong itself; Ramsey led a few men through the village to pick off these stragglers while Japanese fire intensified from across the river. Troops of the 1st Regular Philippine Division soon arrived and the position was secured. Lt Ramsey escaped the Bataan surrender and formed the East-Central Luzon Guerrilla Area. He was later presented the Silver Star and Purple Heart for leading the last charge.
(Inset left) Philippine Department
(Inset right) 26th Cavalry Regiment

Headquarters personnel of a 112th Cavalry troop. The guidons of other branches of service were in their branch colors, but those of the Cavalry retained the long-traditional red over white. On the swallow-tail guidon the regimental number was in white on the red portion, above the troop letter in red on the white portion. (Texas Military Forces Museum)

Texas was still rough and wild in the 1920s–30s, and the 1st/112th Cavalry enforced martial law during the 1918 Longview riot, 1920 Galveston strike, 1928 Borger lawlessness, 1930 Sherman riot, 1931–32 East Texas oilfield lawlessness, 1932 New London School disaster, and 1938 Mexia oilfield lawlessness.

The regiments' 3d Squadrons were inactivated in October 1940 and their two troops reassigned to the other squadrons. On November 18 the Texas NG was Federalized because of the expanding war in Europe; this "limited emergency" call-up was to be for one year, and men were permitted just ten days to get their affairs in order. The brigade, under BrigGen Walter B. Pyron, arrived at Ft Bliss, Texas on the north side of El Paso in the extreme west end of the state; while the cantonment area was in Texas, the vast majority of the post – three times larger than Rhode Island – was in New Mexico.

In February 1941 the brigade was deployed to the Mexican border. The brigade HQ set up in Ft McIntosh outside of Laredo; the 112th, commanded by Col Clarence Parker, relieved the 5th Cavalry at Ft Clark at Brackettville, while the 124th took over from the 12th Cavalry at Ft Brown in Brownsville and Ft Ringgold at Rio Grande City to secure the lower border. In late May the brigade rotated back to Ft Bliss. There the largest massing of cavalry since the Civil War occurred when the six regiments of the brigade and the 1st Cavalry Division and other mounted units conducted a pass-in-review of more than 12,000 men. The brigade participated in the Louisiana Maneuvers in August and September 1941, which made it apparent that cavalry had a difficult time keeping pace with tank units. The 112th returned to Ft Clark in October and remained there until July 1942, when it was relieved by the 9th Cavalry, and began to train for overseas deployment, with the 124th deployed to Ft D.A. Russell. The 7th Cavalry was attached to the brigade from July to September 1942. The 124th prepared for overseas deployment in May 1944. With its units deployed, on May 12, 1944 the brigade HQ Troop became the 56th Cavalry Reconnaissance Troop, Mechanized.

In November 1941 the one-year active duty of the Texas NG units was extended by six months; some men were discharged, others stayed, but then Pearl Harbor was attacked. As soon as these units were Federalized they began to receive fillers and replacements from outside of Texas (for example, the 112th received men from New York, Ohio, Illinois, and elsewhere). There was some friction between the "outsiders" and Texans, but this gradually disappeared. With transfers as cadres and for schooling, the number of Texans dwindled – in Burma the 124th was only 27 percent Texan – but the Texans, coupled with the cavalry traditions, set the units' character.

112th CAVALRY REGIMENT (SPECIAL) 1942–OCTOBER 1944

Rarin' to Go

February 1942 found the regiment at Ft Clark, losing troops and equipment to units deploying overseas, and in May it was itself ordered to prepare for deployment. Its horses were turned over to the relieving 9th Cavalry on July 5, and most of the M1903 Springfield rifles and Colt M1917 revolvers were replaced with M1 rifles and M1911A1 pistols. On July 8 the regiment departed by train for Camp Stoneman, California, retaining all horse equipment and specialists. Arriving on July 12, the regiment undertook conditioning marches, refresher classes, inoculations, and paperwork. Colonel Julian W. Cunningham, a regular, had been reassigned from the 1st Cavalry Division to command the 112th in mid-November 1941. On July 21 the regiment sailed from San Francisco on the SS *President Grant* with 70 officers, two warrants, and 1,476 enlisted men.

On arrival at Nouméa on the French possession of New Caledonia on August 11, the unit was assigned to Sixth Army and attached to 1st Island Command along with the new American Division, to serve as a mobile reserve. The battle for Guadalcanal to the north had just begun; New Caledonia had been scheduled for seizure by the Japanese, but the plan had been abandoned in July after their Midway defeat. Based north of Nouméa, the 112th undertook tactical training and defense exercises. The first shipment of half-wild Australian horses began arriving and by October there were 2,000 more or less broken mounts. It was found that the local grasses provided poor nourishment for them, and feed, fodder, and hay had to be shipped from the States at a time when shipping space was critical. Even with this provision the horses weakened, and it was decided to dismount the only horse cavalry unit sent outside the States. On May 13, 1943, the regiment turned in 1,481 horses and mules and boarded the USS *President Jackson* bound for Townsville, Australia. There were mixed emotions, but most

Texas NG Cavalry, 1940	
56th Cavalry Brigade	
HQ & HQ Troop	San Antonio
112th Cavalry Regiment	
HQ & HQ Tp	Dallas
Machine Gun Tp	Dallas
Medical Detachment	Mineral Wells
Band	Dallas
1st Squadron	Dallas
Tp A	Dallas
Tp B	Dallas
2d Sqn	Dallas
Tp E	Dallas
Tp F	Tyler
3d Sqn	Texarkana
Tp I	Texarkana
Tp K	Abilene
124th Cavalry Regiment	
HQ & HQ Tp	Houston
Machine Gun Tp	San Antonio
Medical Det	Houston
Band	Mineral Wells
1st Sqn	Fort Worth
Tp A	Fort Worth
Tp B	Fort Worth
2d Sqn	Houston
Tp E	Brenham
Tp F	Mineral Wells
3d Sqn	Corpus Christi
Tp I	Corpus Christi
Tp K	Seguin

June 21, 1942: men of the 112th Cavalry embark on the SS *President Grant* at San Francisco, their appearance somewhat different from troops typically departing for the Pacific. The trooper on the right wears M1940 three-buckle boots and the man in the center has the M1931 lace-up type. Lacking duffle bags, they carry their uniforms in blue denim barracks bags. (Texas Military Forces Museum)

LEATHERBACK **Task Force, June–July 1943**
112th Cavalry Regiment
134th Field Artillery Battalion (105mm howitzer)
404th Engineer Company (Combat)
Ordnance Medium Maintenance Co (Provisional)
Co C, 48th Transportation Corps Regt (Truck)
Co B, 481st Quartermaster Port Bn
2d Platoon, 352d QM Bakery Co
67th Fighter Squadron, USAAF (P-39s)
12th Defense Bn, USMC
20th Naval Construction Bn
1st Separate Wire Platoon (USMC)
Administrative unit, USN
Landing craft unit, USN
Argus unit (fighter direction center), USN

troopers – even some of the longtime cavalrymen – were not sad to see their mounts go: they demanded a great deal of care and work, they did not stand up well to the tropical climate and were not suited for jungle warfare. The troopers already realized that they would be fighting on foot; although horses might have provided mobility on less densely vegetated islands, where they were going dense jungles awaited them.

Arriving at Townsville on May 17, the regiment was based at nearby Armstrong Paddock. LEATHERBACK Task Force or Task Force W was established on May 14 with Col Cunningham in command, and the XO, LtCol Alexander M. Miller III, took over the regiment. The task force had the mission of securing undefended Woodlark Island 100 miles northeast of New Guinea's southeastern end. The first echelon departed aboard landing craft, infantry (LCIs) and landed unopposed on Woodlark's southeast coast on June 30; an advance party of engineers had landed on the 23rd. The task force secured the island and established a perimeter allowing Seabees to construct an airfield; the only action was single-bomber night harassing raids. The regiment undertook additional training to include amphibious landings with rubber boats.

NEW BRITAIN

On November 30, 1943 the 112th arrived at Goodenough Island north of New Guinea to prepare for its part in the New Britain campaign, for which DIRECTOR Task Force was formed under comand of BrigGen Cunningham. The plan was for the Marines to make the main landing on the island's west end, almost 400 miles from the Japanese base of Rabaul at the opposite end; as a diversion the 112th would land at Cape Merkus 11 days prior to the main Marine landing at Cape Gloucester 100 miles to the northwest.

On Goodenough the officers and support troops received M1 carbines, and a BAR and a Thompson SMG were issued to each squad; while the squads had M1 rifles each retained one M1903 with a grenade launcher. The regiment also received a number of bazookas, and four flamethrowers.

It was on Woodlark that the 112th began to be informally called the 112th Cavalry Regimental Combat Team, with BrigGen Cunningham in command and Col Miller commanding the regiment. Two units were attached to the 112th Cavalry RCT. The 148th Field Artillery Battalion began life as 1st Bn, 148th Field Artillery Regt (75mm Gun) of the Idaho National Guard. Inducted into Federal service in September 1940, it was shipped to Australia intended to reinforce the Philippines; this plan was canceled, and in February 1942 the battalion was attached to an Australian force sent to defend Timor, but the Japanese seized the island before the convoy arrived. The battalion

The color guard of the 112th Cavalry on New Caledonia, 1942. Cavalry regimental colors were yellow and emblazoned with the regimental crest and motto – in this case, *Rarin' to Go*. (Texas Military Forces Museum)

was redesignated the 148th Field Artillery Bn on June 17, 1942 and received 12× 105mm M2A1 howitzers in February 1943. It had served with the 158th Infantry on Kiriwina Island before joining the 112th. The other unit was the 59th Engineer Company, activated December 19, 1942 in the Panama Canal Zone; it would be detached from the 112th and reorganized and redesignated on September 22, 1944 as the 59th Engineer Service Company.

The task force departed Goodenough on December 14 to land on New Britain the next day – Z-Day. Cape Merkus was defended by only 120 Japanese soldiers and sailors, but these may have been increased to 500 by the time of the landing, and a Japanese battalion was located 11 miles northeast of the Cape. In the pre-dawn hours of December 15, Troops A and B, 1/112th Cavalry embarked on rubber boats from destroyer-transports, to land at Umtingalu village east of the Arawe peninsula and on the northeast shore of Pilelo Island south of Cape Merkus, respectively. When Troop A's 15-man boats were 35–100 yards offshore just before dawn they were engaged by heavy automatic fire and all but three were shredded; while only 12 men were killed, four missing, and 17 wounded, the troop was rendered ineffective owing to lost weapons, equipment, and even uniforms. Troop B in fact landed on the northwest shore of Pilelo at 0530hrs, moving to the island's north end and destroying a Japanese radio site. In the meantime the 2d Sqn entered Arawe harbour and landed on Beach Orange aboard Marine amphibious tractors at 0730hrs, meeting light resistance; the peninsula was cleared and 1,600 men got ashore.

The Japanese withdrew eastwards, launching several mostly unsuccessful air attacks against Arawe over the following weeks. Two Japanese battalions began closing in on the beachhead, but the terrain and rain-swollen streams so slowed them that they did not arrive until December 26 and 29, by which time 4,750 US troops were ashore and conducting aggressive patrols. A defensive perimeter established at the base of the peninsula presented a 1,700-yard front to the Japanese, who dug in to the east of it. The Arawe

A 112th Cavalry pack train after receiving horses from Australia. Each troop and headquarters unit had a small pack train to transport unit equipment and forage, which is seen here in large sacks – in effect, this was the troop's "fuel" transport element. (Texas Military Forces Museum)

Troops A and B, 112th Cavalry, undertook rubber boat training at Goodenough Island in December 1943, using 15-man LCR(L)s. Both troops attempted to land in rubber boats at Cape Merkus, New Britain on December 15, with disastrous results for Troop A. (Texas Military Forces Museum)

landing was successful in that it tied down two enemy battalions that could have been used against the main Cape Gloucester landing, and attracted Japanese aircraft that were often destroyed by US air cover.

In the meantime the 1st Marine Div landed at Cape Gloucester as planned on December 26 and made slow but steady headway. At Arawe the Americans and Japanese probed one another until January 16, when an American attack drove off the enemy. That same day a Marine patrol from Cape Gloucester linked up with a 112th patrol, and the Japanese command at Rabaul ordered all units to pull back to the redoubt on January 23. The 112th remained in the Arawe area until relieved by elements of the 40th Inf Div in June. The regiment suffered 72 killed, 142 wounded, and four missing. There was a conflict with Sixth Army which was reluctant to award the 112th the Combat Infantryman's Badge, but this was resolved.

Troopers of the 112th Cavalry load into an LCVP (Landing Craft, Vehicle and Personnel – this early model lacks the pair of aft machine-gun tubs) prior to landing at Arawe Harbour, New Britain on December 15, 1943. The men carry olive drab jungle backpacks. (Texas Military Forces Museum)

NEW GUINEA

On June 9, 1944 the 112th arrived at Finschhafen, New Guinea for rest and training, but on the 24th – far sooner than anticipated – the regiment was alerted for movement to Aitape further west up New Guinea's northern coast. The rifle troops were 10–20 men understrength and, more importantly, they were worn out after six months in the New Britain jungle. They arrived at Aitape on June 28 and immediately headed into the jungle, leaving behind 37mm guns, 81mm mortars and bazookas; the weapon crews reorganized as rifle platoons and ammunition bearers (three 81mm mortars were later airdropped to the regiment).

US forces had landed at Aitape in late April 1944 at the same time as another landing 125 miles further west at Hollandia. Just under 100 miles to the east of Aitape was Wewak, and in this area the Japanese Eighteenth Army had been bypassed, splitting the Japanese forces strung along the northern coast. Now 35,000 Eighteenth Army troops were marching west in an effort to fight their way through Aitape and then Hollandia to rejoin Second Area Army in western New Guinea, and some 20,000 Japanese were left at Wewak as a rearguard.

XI Corps established a covering force line on the Driniumor River 15 miles east of Aitape, stretching 13 miles from the coast across the flat, jungled coastal plain to the inland mountains. The river was only a couple of feet deep and offered no obstacle other than an open field of fire. The defenders were designated PERSECUTION Covering Force; the 32d Inf Div held most of the line, and the 112th Cavalry was positioned on the right inland flank. The 32d Div had incorporated the 112th into the defense based on the assumption that it was a 3,000-man infantry regiment; instead it received a 1,500-man, two-squadron regiment. The 2d Sqn was positioned forward on the river, which it reached on July 1, with the 1st Sqn 2½ miles to the rear with a back-up position on an unnamed "River X." The 112th's 148th Field Artillery was left in the rear, and the 120th Field Artillery on the coast supported the 112th from afar.

Defenses were prepared and extensive patrols pushed eastward; it rained incessantly, ammunition and rations were limited, and most resupply was

---

D MORTAR SUPPORT ON THE DRINIUMOR: 112th CAVALRY, JULY 1944

At Arawe the 112th Cavalry initially deployed only six of its 12× 60mm M2 mortars, mainly to conserve manpower. Officially two were assigned to the mortar section in rifle troop weapon platoons; instead, three mortars were kept under squadron control and on occasion all six were under regimental control. To give them a job, unit farriers (horse-shoers) were retrained as mortarmen when the regiment converted to dismounted. One of a squadron's three mortars would be positioned forward to fire illumination rounds for the outpost line forward of the main line of resistance, while the others supported by firing barrages into pre-designated "boxes." The mortars proved more effective than envisioned, and could engage targets faster than artillery. By the time of the Aitape operation and the defense of the Driniumor in June–July the regiment had manned all 12 of its mortars; they would still sometimes concentrate the 60mm mortars under squadron or regimental control to augment the 81mm mortars. On the Driniumor the mortars proved invaluable for quickly engaging sudden enemy rushes across the broad, shallow river. The 42lb 60mm had a minimum range of 100 yards and a maximum of 1,985 yards. When the regiment occupied its defensive positions the troopers carried in 50 rounds per tube, but all resupply was by airdrop. The normal sustained rate of fire was 18 rounds per minute, but it could pop out 30-35rpm in an emergency, and 60mm fire could be brought in as close as 30 yards from friendly positions. Both high-explosive and illumination rounds were available, and white phosphorous smoke rounds from 1944. The burn duration of the parachute-suspended illumination rounds was about 25 seconds.

(Inset) 112th Cavalry Regiment

December 15, 1943: 2d Sqn, 112th Cavalry coming ashore at Arawe Harbour. Prior to the landing the rifle squads were up-gunned by issuing each a .30cal M1918A2 BAR and a .45cal M1 Thompson submachine gun – a significant firepower increase over just eight M1 rifles. (Texas Military Forces Museum)

delivered by airdrop. The Japanese were half starved, exhausted after a long march over rugged terrain, and poorly armed, but they were determined, having no other choice than to push on – behind them were only depleted ration depots and equally determined Australians. As their 20th and 41st Divs closed in on the Driniumor, contacts increased. The Japanese planned a main attack just south of the coast; one force would attack westward and another would swing south to attack the southern portion of the line held by the 112th. On July 10 the 2d Sqn moved east a couple of miles across the river for a reconnaissance-in-force, and the 1st Sqn moved up to occupy its Driniumor positions.

The Japanese struck on the night of July 10/11, attacking through dense jungle in the dark; three understrength regiments penetrated the 128th Infantry line and two swung south towards the 112th. A general withdrawal to River X commenced, but the 112th concentrated in its position on the Driniumor and held out against attacks from all directions. The seesaw battle went on for days, characterized by repeated counterattacks and counter-movements by both sides; most of the time the 112th was cut off and resupplied by airdrop. The Driniumor defense line was gradually reestablished, but the 112th on the flank continued to be attacked from all directions. During vicious hand-to-hand fighting a platoon leader of Troop E, 2nd Lt Dale E. Christensen, crept through enemy lines, knocking out machine-gun nests and leading numerous counterattacks until he was killed; he was awarded the Medal of Honor. A second Medal of Honor was earned by 2nd Lt George W.G. Boyce, Jr of Troop A when he threw himself on a grenade to protect his men.

The opposing sides regrouped on July 20. While the 112th was strung out along hundreds of yards of the Driniumor, the Japanese concentrated their whole reduced 20th Div against the extreme southern flank. Troop C of the 112th was surrounded for three days and the regimental command was uncertain if it survived. Every available man was thrown into action, and a Provisional Squadron was scraped up from the regimental Weapons and Services Troops. From July 12 the 112th RCT and 3d Bn, 127th Infantry were designated the Southern Force. By the end of July the regiment had lost more than 270 men. Up to this point the Southern Force had been on the defensive; on July 22 the complete 127th Infantry was attached to it, and Cunningham commenced his counteroffensive on August 1. To the north, US battalions were driving across the river while the 112th was still under attack, and the tide began to turn, despite a drastic rate of casualties and evacuations due to illness. By this time the two Japanese divisions fielded only a few hundred effectives, and the morale of the worn-out US troopers lifted on August 4 when it became clear that the enemy was almost spent. Patrols were dispatched to cut off retreating Japanese from August 5, and the last casualty was suffered on the 8th. On August 11 the regiment marched to the mouth of the Driniumor to meet trucks for Aitape. The 112th had suffered 317 combat casualties and hundreds more from illness and fatigue. They had killed more than 1,600 Japanese. War correspondents dubbed the unit the "Little Giant of the Pacific"; Sixth Army officers came to call it "Baldy Force," after BrigGen Cunningham's most immediately noticeable characteristic.

The regiment was rebuilt at Aitape and reorganized, with "(Special)" being appended to its designation on October 1. The 112th RCT designation and structure were made official, with a 50-man RCT HQ; the 3296th Signal Service Platoon was added, and each squadron received a weapons troop

A wounded 112th Cavalry trooper is treated at a squadron aid station on New Britain; apparently a broken leg is being set. (Texas Military Forces Museum)

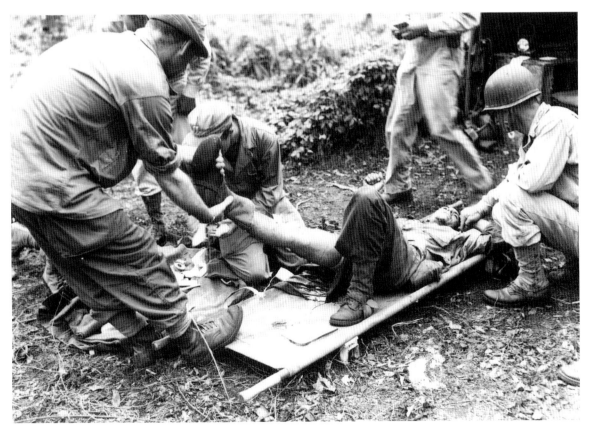

112th Cavalry troopers buying bananas from Filipinas on Luzon, 1945. Note the full-color regimental crest painted on their M1 steel helmets – see Plate D for colors. (Texas Military Forces Museum)

(D and H). Some 600 replacements arrived from the inactivated 816th Tank Destroyer Bn, but these men totally lacked infantry training.

On October 31, 1944 the 112th RCT boarded the USS *Frederick Funston* bound for Leyte in the Philippines – where the main US landings had taken place on October 20 – with stops at Hollandia and Morotai Island. It landed on Leyte on November 14, with a field strength of 137 officers and 2,305 enlisted men (out of an authorized establishment of 153 and 2,474). Upon arrival the 112th Cavalry RCT was attached to the 1st Cavalry Division and would remain so, including for the Luzon campaign and the occupation of Japan; the regiment's actions thereafter are noted in the 1st Cav Div chapter below. Besides two Medals of Honor, members of the regiment were presented 177 other medals for valor while suffering 224 killed in action and over 1,000 wounded in 434 days of combat. They killed an estimated 7,200 Japanese.

124th CAVALRY REGIMENT (SPECIAL) 1942–45

Golpeo Rapidemente (I Strike Quickly)

The 124th was stationed at Ft D.A. Russell in November 1941, returning to Ft Brown in December 1943, and by that late stage many believed that they would see out the war on the Mexican border. However, on May 12, 1944 the regiment was alerted for overseas deployment and relocated to Ft Riley, Kansas under Col Milo H. Matteson, who had taken command the month before. The 124th traveled by train with all its horses and cavalry equipment;

The commander and staff of the 124th Cavalry in India prior to setting out for Burma. While the regiment are training to fight as infantry in the forested hills of Burma, there is little doubt here of the unit's cavalry origins. (Texas Military Forces Museum)

the animals were then turned in, but the unit took its equipment when it entrained for Camp Anza, California in July. Although assigned a New York Army Post Office number, which meant deployment to Europe, they were heading to a port of embarkation for the Pacific, or specifically the China-Burma-India (CBI) Theater. Loaded aboard the USS *General H.W.Butner*, the 124th departed Los Angeles on July 25 bound for India; they arrived on August 26 at Bombay and then went by rail to Ramgarh Training Center near Ranchi. The 124th Cavalry was officially dismounted

The 124th Cavalry could not have accomplished its mission to open the Burma Road without the aid of pack mules, and the Quartermaster pack transport troops required just as much training as combat troops. Trail discipline, pack-saddle loading and unloading for different types of cargo, balancing ever-changing loads, and the care and feeding of the mules were all essential skills. (Texas Military Forces Museum)

Pack mules are led through a trench system overlooking the Burma Road; the rectangular cans on the Phillips pack saddles each contain four 81mm mortar rounds. The height of the ridges the 124th had to climb is dramatized here by the fact that at top left in this photo a C-47 can just be seen flying well below them. (Texas Military Forces Museum)

and reorganized between September 20 and 25, 1944, and was redesignated "(Special)." A 3d Squadron was activated, with men transferred into leadership and specialty positions from the other two.

The regiment now learned that they were destined to serve as a long-range penetration unit that would operate behind Japanese lines in north Burma, taking over the mission of the now disbanded "Merrill's Marauders" – the 5307th Composite Unit, Provisional. Some of the Marauders were absorbed into the new 475th Infantry Regiment (Long Range Penetration, Special), which would be the 124th's partner. Upon arrival in India the regiment numbered 78 officers and 1,522 enlisted men; the new table of organization called for 100 officers and 2,047 enlisted, making it the largest wartime cavalry regiment, dismounted or not. But while the 475th Infantry was authorized 3,049 men, the 124th Cavalry – regardless of its new 3d Sqn – was authorized only 2,073; the three squadrons each had 20 officers and 495 enlisted. (While they had the same mission, the regiment was also denied the "Long Range Penetration" title borne by the 475th.) Six hundred infantry replacements expected from the States went instead to the 475th, so cavalry officers trawled Calcutta replacement depots, but most of the fillers they recruited were service troops with no combat training beyond basic. There were no squadron weapons troops as in other regiments, perhaps simply because the manpower was unavailable, though squadrons did have an intelligence and reconnaissance platoon.

When the 124th departed Ramgarh it numbered just 101 officers and 1,756 enlisted; they had undertaken infantry, jungle, and patrol training along with a great deal of live-fire and forced marches, and instruction in the mission and techniques of long-range penetration units as developed by the British Chindits. It took two weeks by rail and air to reach Myitkyina, Burma, 300 miles north of Mandalay, where the Burma Road to China originated. At Camp Landis north of Myitkyina the 124th joined the in-place 475th Infantry within the MARS Task Force – 5332d Brigade (Provisional), known as the "Marsmen of Burma," or the "New Galahad," in reference to the codename of the former Marauders ("MARS" was said to stand for "Merrills And ReplacementS"). The brigade, formed on July 26, 1944 under BrigGen Thomas S. Arms, was subordinate to the Northern Combat Area Command, which also controlled Chinese divisions. (Arms was injured on October 31 and BrigGen John P. Willey took over command.)

The 613th Field Artillery Bn, with 12× 75mm M1A1 pack howitzers, had been activated at Camp Gruber, Oklahoma in February 1943, training at Ft Carson, Colorado before being shipped to India; it was assigned 445 men and 347 mules. The pack transport troops, without which the Force could not have accomplished its mission, averaged 200 mules, with a troop attached to each 124th squadron. The 7th Chinese Animal Transport Co, with 100 Tonga ponies, was split to carry the surgical hospitals. The Kachin Rangers, trained by the OSS, were local mountain tribesmen serving as scouts and guides. A battery of the 613th was normally attached to each 124th squadron, as were a pack transport troop and a Kachin platoon, to form squadron combat teams. (The 475th Infantry generally kept its artillery under central control.)

Colonel Thomas J. Heavey assumed command of the 124th in November 1944 and remained until January 1945; after he succumbed to the rigors of the march

(continued on page 36)

5332d Brigade (Provisional), July 1944–May 1945

HQ & HQ Company, 5332d Bde

124th Cav Regt (Special)

613th Field Arty Bn (75mm pack)

49th Medical Portable Surgical Hospital

37th, 252d, 253d QM Pack Transport Tps

one-half, 7th Chinese Animal Transport Co

16× teams, CBI War Dog Detachment

3× Kachin Ranger platoons

475th Inf Regt (Long-Range Penetration, Special)

612th Field Arty Bn (75mm pack)

44th MPS Hospital

31st, 33d, 35th QM Pack Transport Tps

one-half, 7th Chinese Animal Transport Co

16× teams, CBI War Dog Detachment

3× Kachin Ranger plats

1st Chinese Infantry Regt (Separate)*

42d Medical Portable Surgical Hospital (US)

18th Veterinary Evacuation Hospital

Co B, 13th Mountain Medical Bn

511th Medical Collecting Co

2× Japanese language translation/ interrogation teams

India Detachment, Tp B, 252d QM Remount Sqn (at Ramgarh Trg Center)

699th QM Remount Tp (at Ledo Forward Remount Depot)

* Released to 50th Chinese Div on February 13, 1945, this 2,631-man unit never fought alongside 5332d Bde.

Mules ready to be loaded with supplies from a resupply airdrop. Such drops occurred every three days, weather and suitable clearings permitting, but this was not predictable. (Texas Military Forces Museum)

An 81mm M1 mortar crew service their weapon; the 124th Cavalry possessed only four of these mortars. The man swabbing the bore carries a jungle first-aid kit and M3 trench knife on his pistol belt. The gauntness of these troopers demonstrates their short rations and the loss of most body fat through endless strenuous marching and activity. (Texas Military Forces Museum)

ON THE TRAIL IN BURMA: 124th CAVALRY, JANUARY 1945

The 124th Cavalry of the MARS Task Force had a Quartermaster pack transport troop of approximately 200 mules and "muleskinners" ("So mean and hard they could skin a mule alive") – or "packers" or "mule drivers", officially called "mule handlers." The mules were essential for transporting crew-served weapons, crew-served and individual ammunition reserves, rations (airdropped every three days, weather permitting), radios, medical supplies, unit equipment, and all other material. The M1924 Phillips pack saddle, a design dating back to Indian-fighting days, could be configured in a number of different ways and was provided with a variety of attachments and containers to adapt it to different loads of over 200lb (plus the 90lb saddle). A muleskinner was required to possess a great depth of knowledge on packing, rigging, and mule care. Their charges were commonly known as "hay-burners," "jarheads" (a jar being empty), "jugheads," "hardheads," and less-repeatable names. It was not unusual for ill and exhausted troopers to hang their jungle backpack and even their weapon on a mule's load, at least until the lieutenant came down the line. These jungle packs, in both olive drab and camouflage versions, were issued to other dismounted cavalry units from 1944. Besides M1 rifles and carbines the Marsmen were also issued .45cal M3 submachine guns ("grease guns"). A rifle squadron with a howitzer battery carrying broken-down 75mm M1A1 pack howitzers ("jackass guns"), pack transport troop, Kachin Scout platoon, and other small attachments numbered almost 1,000 men and nearly 300 mules. Including designated gaps between units to reduce start-and-stop movement, the column would be strung out for almost 3,000 yards on a winding mountain trail. The ration situation was much better for the MARS Task Force than it had been for the half-starved Merrill's Marauders; the Marauders had subsisted only on K-rations for months – a distribution schedule slavishly adhered to by logistics officers who ignored the poor health conditions and the tremendous expenditure of energy required over a prolonged period. The Marsmen additionally received C-rations, rice, canned fruit and juices, and other supplements to nourish them in the brutal conditions and punishing terrain.

(Inset) 124th Cavalry Regiment

Col William L. Osborne, commander of the 475th Infantry, took temporary command until February 1945, when Col Lorean D. Pegg took over the 124th until June 1945.

The 5332nd Bde's mission was to complete the opening of the Burma Road from Myitkyina into China to provide an overland supply route to the Nationalist Chinese (at that stage all supplies for China had to be flown over "the Hump" of the eastern Himalaya Mountains – costly in aircraft, crews, and fuel, and carrying inadequate payloads). The brigade was to open the section of the Burma Road under Japanese control near Hosi. The formation began to assemble in September; its growing pains were difficult due to manpower shortages and limited training time, although equipment was plentiful.

ADVANCE FROM MYITKYINA

Between October 15 and 17, 1944 the 475th departed by foot, heading southwest then south; the Chinese regiment soon followed. The 124th departed only on December 16, moving south to Momauk on the Stillwell Road; the regiment had unavoidably been delayed by the need for training which the 475th had already received. The regiment was to move on jungle trails through the mountains to Mong Wi, where the brigade would assemble between the sectors held by the Japanese 18th and 49th Divs; it was suspected that the Japanese might retreat through Mong Wi.

Vehicles and other heavy gear were left behind, and everything was carried on the cavalrymen's backs or by mule; like the Marauders, they would rely for their rations, animal feed, ammunition, and other supplies on airdrops every three days. There were a few unauthorized mule- and local pony-carts, and the 124th initially took along two Japanese trucks and a few jeeps, not knowing how far they would be able to travel, but these were abandoned as they trekked into the mountains. At the beginning of January 1945 the rains began, turning the mountain trails into dangerous mudslides. The regiment reached the Shweli River at Mong Hkak on January 9; the rain let up, and the column was finally resupplied. After a rest it headed for Mong Wi further east and over more mountains; there, after covering 279 miles over 7,800ft

An ammunition dump established behind the 124th Cavalry's positions overlooking the embattled Burma Road. Every single item had to be delivered by airdrop, brought to the dump by mule, and carried forward by mule, or sometimes even man-packed. (Texas Military Forces Museum)

mountains, the 124th linked up with the 475th Infantry on January 12. (The Japanese explained the sudden appearance of such a large force by reporting them as paratroopers, a perception reinforced by the supply parachute drops.)

The 475th was sent east to the Burma Road on January 13; it was intended that the 124th secure Mong Wi as a base, but since Northern China Combat Area refused to release the 1st Chinese Regt to the brigade the troopers were also ordered forward on the 15th. The unit was to advance around the 475th's left flank and move ahead to Kawngsong on the Burma Road. The rains continued, resupply drops were impossible, and the weather and the forested hills were disorienting. The brigade had been directed to keep casualties down, to harass the Japanese with nuisance attacks and roadblocks but not to become decisively engaged. The 475th established a base at Nawhkan about 2 miles west of the Burma Road and north of Hosi; the 3/124th was just to its north, in close contact with the Japanese, and prepared to launch its attack on the Japanese 4th Regt, 2nd Div on January 19. (The 30th Chinese Div was attacking further to the north.)

On the 19th the 475th cratered the road with demolitions, while the 3/124th suffered a great deal of heavy artillery and mortar fire until the 613th Field Artillery was concentrated and suppressed the Japanese artillery. The regiment-sized Yamakazi Detachment then arrived to reinforce the defense, but on the morning of the 20th the 3d Sqn secured its objective and was joined by 1/124th. Mines, boobytraps, artillery, and ambushes on the road were not halting Japanese traffic on the main supply route for their 56th Div further north, but despite repeated requests the brigade was not permitted to actually occupy the road. The cavalrymen discovered and blew up a large Japanese ammunition dump; they cleared the area around their positions, but as they were not permitted to place themselves squarely across the road they

November 1944: the remaining Texans from Mineral Wells, assigned to Troop F, 124th Cavalry. Visible weapons include M1 rifles and M1 carbines, plus a single .45cal M3 SMG "grease gun" held by the second man from right, second row. (Texas Military Forces Museum)

were unable to prevent its use by the Japanese through the end of the month. During that time the Japanese were able to keep the 56th Div supplied, albeit while suffering losses, and then to withdraw it down the road; all efforts by the Chinese to trap and destroy it failed due to the command confusion in regards to actually cutting the road.

The last major action of the 124th was an effort to secure defended high ground at Hpa-pen closer to the road in conjunction with the 88th Regt, 30th Chinese Div. The 2/124th moved north to an assembly area on the night of February 1 prepared for the next day's attack, which the Chinese wished to postpone; the attack was launched, and resistance was very heavy. First Lieutenant Jack L. Knight of Troop F made repeated one-man attacks on enemy positions even though he was wounded and saw his brother killed; he finally died while dragging himself to another position, and was posthumously awarded the Medal of Honor. That hill was secured with a loss of 22 dead. February 3 saw the 475th Infantry's last major action, but patrols, ambushes, and skirmishes continued until February 10 when the Japanese had mostly withdrawn from the area. The 124th lost 64 dead and 277 wounded in the campaign.

MARS Force established an administrative bivouac, and large numbers of troops were evacuated due to illness and fatigue. On February 28 the 124th began a 50-mile march south on the Burma Road to Lashio; there the 1st and 2d Sqns each formed a provisional truck troop, and the 3d Sqn three. From there the regiment was flown to Kunming, China between April 26 and May 14, 1945. For the most part the units provided logistics support for the Chinese Combat Command, which was actually a training and logistical organization. Many men simply found jobs with the various American

124th Cavalry troopers at an assembly area. The relaxed wear of fatigues and field caps was the norm in Burma. (Texas Military Forces Museum)

training and support units within the command, and the small numbers of remaining Texans inducted with the regiment in 1940 were rotated home. "MARS Force" was disbanded in late May 1945, and on June 26 orders were received to inactivate the 124th Cavalry on July 1. The remaining troops were officially reassigned to a wide variety of duties in the Chinese Combat Command, Chinese Training Command, Chinese and American Services of Supply, OSS, and other organizations.

1st CAVALRY DIVISION (SPECIAL)

The First Team

As mentioned above, the Army's only active cavalry division had been activated on September 13, 1921 at Ft Bliss, Texas with the 1st, 7th, 8th, and 10th Cavalry, though it would not be until the next year that all assigned units arrived at their stations. The assignment of the Colored 10th Cavalry to a white formation violated regulations and it was replaced by the 5th in 1922. The 1st Bde was detached to Douglas, Arizona; the division was responsible for the security of the Arizona, New Mexico, and Texas borders with Mexico, and was assigned to the VIII Corps Area. In 1923 the division moved to Marfa in the Texas Big Bend region for divisional maneuvers. For the next four years divisional elements were stationed at Ft Bliss, Camp Marfa, and Ft Clark, chasing smugglers, patrolling the border, and conducting training. Another divisional maneuver was conducted in 1928, the year the division received its first motorized vehicles. The 1st Cavalry Regt was replaced by the 12th in 1933; additional division maneuvers were conducted in 1933, 1938, and 1939.

With war in Europe and turmoil in China, training intensified. The Texas National Guard's Federalized 56th Cav Bde was attached to the division in 1940. Each regiment's two squadrons received a third troop (C and G). Alternating between training and border security, the division took part in three major Louisiana maneuvers in August 1940, August-October 1941, and

July–September 1942. The division was concentrated at Ft Bliss in early 1941, with MajGen Innis P. Swift in command from April. After Pearl Harbor the division, assigned to the Southern Defense Command with 56th Cav Bde, feared that it would be left out of the war and condemned to border surveillance, as had happened in World War I. Before long 1,250 experienced NCOs and troopers were sent as cadre to organize the 91st Inf Div, which suggested an even worse fate for the division – to be simply a manpower pool. However, while a reconnaissance squadron, artillery battalion, and engineer squadron were sent away, the divisional support units were fully motorized and the division was subsequently brought up to full war strength in both personnel and equipment. Besides the two Texas NG regiments, many troops of the divisional regiments were also from Texas and other southwestern states.

In February 1943 the "1st Cav" was alerted for deployment to the Pacific. There was a rush to find copies of jungle warfare manuals, which were simply read to officers and NCOs seated in sweltering desert classrooms – there was no place to conduct jungle training in barren west Texas. At the same time the division was informed that it would be dismounted, which officially took place on February 23.[5] This necessitated personnel changes owing to the numbers of saddlers (leather repairers), stablemen, farriers, veterinary personnel, and other specialists. The cavalry regiments would not be mechanized but would fight on foot; there were internal reorganizations and much new equipment was issued. Cadres sent to new units, OCS volunteers, and transfers to the Army Air Forces began to draw away cavalrymen, and the formation received recruits, specialists, and newly commissioned officers unfamiliar with cavalry traditions.

OVERSEAS AT LAST

Divided into two movement echelons, the division traveled by rail to Camp Stoneman, California in May and June 1943. The 5th Cavalry and 8th Engineer Sqn departed San Francisco on July 2 and arrived at Brisbane, Australia on the 24th. On the 26th the division was assigned to Sixth Army, the "Alamo Force" under MajGen Walther Krueger, beginning construction on Camp Startpine 15 miles north of Brisbane with the aid of Australian contractors. The 7th and 8th Cavalry departed San Francisco on June 26 and arrived at Brisbane on July 11; the 12th departed on July 3 and arrived on the 24th (the division was shipped aboard the SS *Monterey* and SS *George Washington*). The nearby town of Pine Rivers, population 4,800, was

---

1st Cavalry Division (Special), 1942–45

(1942 strength: 12,112 troops, 7,298 horses, 1,182 trucks)

HQ & HQ Troop, 1st Cav Div

HQ & HQ Tp, 1st Cav Bde

    5th Cav Regt

    12th Cav Regt

HQ & HQ Tp, 2d Cav Bde

    7th Cav Regt

    8th Cav Regt

HQ & HQ Battery, 1st Cav Div

    61st Field Artillery Bn[1]

    82d Field Artillery Bn[2]

    99th Field Artillery Bn[3]

    271st Field Artillery Bn[4]

    947th Field Artillery Bn[5]

1st Medical Sqn

7th Reconnaissance Sqn[6]

8th Engineer Sqn

16th QM Sqn

1st Signal Tp

27th Ordnance Medium Maintenance Co

302d Recon Tp (Mechanized)[6]

603d Medium Tank Co[7]

801st Counter Intelligence Corps Det

Military Police Platoon, 1st Cav Div

Notes:
(1) 105mm M3 pack until converted to M2A1 in Oct 1943. Trucks replaced by TD-9 dozer-tractors in Jan 1944.
(2) 75mm pack jeep-drawn until converted to 105mm M2A1 in Oct 1944. Jeeps replaced by 3/4-ton trucks in Jan 1944.
(3) Replaced 62d Field Arty in 1942, originally mule pack; 75mm pack jeep-drawn until converted to 105mm M2A1 in July 1945. Jeeps replaced by 3/4-ton trucks in Jan 1944.
(4) Organized in Australia in Oct 1943; 105mm M2A1. Trucks replaced by TD-9 dozer-tractors in Jan 1944.
(5) Attached Oct 1944, assigned Jan 1945; 155mm M1A1 howitzers.
(6) Sqn attached Jan 1942-Dec 1943; replaced by 302d Recon Troop, which designated Mechanized in Oct 1944.
(7) Co designated Light prior to Dec 1943.

---

5 Some 6,750 horses and 300 mules were turned in. Contrary to a myth created by the 1995 movie *In Pursuit of Honor*, the Army did not order the killing of surplus horses; the Treasury Dept auctioned them to civilians in 1944.

quite overwhelmed by the 15,000 cavalrymen. Once the camp was completed the division undertook six months of jungle warfare training in subtropical Queensland, and amphibious training at nearby Moreton Bay, Toorbul Point near Brisbane, and Port Stephens in New South Wales.

At Startpine the 7th Recon Sqn was split into a reconnaissance troop and a light tank company (within the recon troop was a small group of Sioux Indian radiomen employed similarly to the Marines' Navajo code-talkers). A battalion of 105mm howitzers was organized to augment the truck-drawn 75mm pack howitzer battalions. On December 4 the regiments underwent further organizational and equipment modifications to prepare them for

February 29, 1944: troopers of the 2d Sqn, 5th Cavalry land in Hyane Harbour on the east side of Los Negros Island in the Admiralties. (US Army)

The central portion of Los Negros, with the pale streak of Momote airfield to the immediate left of Hyane Harbour bay. The arrow marks the landing site, and the black line the approximate initial trace of the BREWER Task Force perimeter around the airfield. The Japanese expected the American landing to be in Seeadler Harbour in the upper portion, and on the shores of the larger Manus Island. (US Army)

BREWER **Task Force, February–March 1944**
Reconnaissance Force
Detachment, HQ & HQ Tp, 1st Cavalry Bde
2d Sqn, 5th Cav Regt
673d AA MG Bty (Airborne)
Recon Plat, HQ Tp, 1st Cav Bde
Communications Platoon, HQ Tp, 1st Cav Bde
1st Plat, Tp B (Clearing), 1st Medical Sqn
30th Medical Surgical Hospital (Portable)
Naval Gunfire Support Party, USN
12th Air Liaison Party, USAAF
Detachment, Australian-New Guinea Admin Unit (porters)
Support Force
5th Cav Regt (–2d Sqn)
99th Field Arty Bn (-two sections)
40th Naval Construction Bn
1st Collecting Tp, 1st Medical Sqn
Bty C, 168th AAA Bn (90mm Gun)
Bty C, 211th AAA Bn (Automatic Wpns)
Co E, Shore Bn, 592d Engineer Boat & Shore Regt
1st Plat, Tp A, 8th Engineer Sqn

infantry action; this included adding a weapons troop for each squadron (Troops D and H); the division was redesignated the 1st Cavalry Division (Special) and "(Special)" was appended to the regimental designations on that date.

Between January 22 and 26, 1944 the division shipped to Cape Sudest at Oro Bay on the north coast of New Guinea. On the 27th the 1,026-man first echelon of BREWER Task Force sailed off on the division's first combat operation under command of BrigGen William C. Chase, 1st Bde commander. The task force was bound for Los Negros in the Admiralty Islands 200 miles northeast of New Guinea; Los Negros and the larger adjacent Manus Island were needed for air and naval bases in the effort to neutralize Rabaul, the area's main Japanese base complex some 390 miles away.

THE ADMIRALTY ISLANDS

There was a great deal of disagreement over Japanese strength, with the Army Air Forces claiming that the islands had been largely evacuated while Army estimates were between 4,000 and 5,000 troops; in reality 4,450 well-camouflaged defenders had been refraining from firing on aircraft. The Los Negros landing strategy was different from any other. Most operations put a large assault force ashore prepared to seize the island, but because of the uncertainty over Los Negros even being occupied only a 1,000-man reconnaissance-in-force would land, with three options: (1) if undefended, to secure the airfield and landing site;

The fighting on Los Negros and Manus was brutal, and the difficulties were amplified by the hot, humid climate. This exhausted trooper wears a worn lightweight wool knit shirt, as used in both warm and cold weather. Note the M3 trench knives and rubber dog-tag silencers. (US Army)

Filipino civilians fleeing the Japanese are passed through 1st Cavalry Division lines. Individuals in rifle troops had red-and-white checkered marker panels on their backs to enable supporting weapon crews to observe their advance; they would bend over to reveal their backs when US aircraft flew overhead. (US Army)

(2) if heavily defended, to withdraw and await a stronger landing force; (3) if moderately defended, to establish a foothold and await reinforcement by the Support Force two days later. Other than it being an amphibious landing and without horses, this could thus be described as a traditional cavalry mission.

The task force departed Cape Sudest on February 27 to land on the 29th. The 2d Sqn, 5th Cavalry (2/5 Cav) landed in enclosed Hyane bay on Los Negros' east coast; the Japanese, deployed to defend the northern shoreline, were taken completely by surprise. The airfield was overrun and Gen MacArthur, who had accompanied the force as an observer, came ashore to assess whether the cavalrymen could hold; on departing he directed the Support Force and the rest of the division to make all haste. The troopers pulled back to a point of land with their backs to the sea and the Japanese had to attack across the airfield; this tight defensive line held against repeated attacks, and the Support Force arrived on March 4. The 12th Cavalry landed on the island's northern arm on the 6th; the 2d Cav Bde under BrigGen Verne D. Mudge arrived on the 9th, and secured the small adjacent islands over the following days, landing on Manus on March 15 to secure the airfield there. Los Negros was not completely cleared until March 25, and Manus during May. In a long, grueling series of small unit actions and patrols almost 4,400 Japanese were killed and 75 prisoners taken, at a cost to the 1st Cav of 290 killed, four missing, and 977 wounded. Sergeant Troy A. McGill of the 5th Cavalry was awarded the Medal of Honor for single-handedly defending his position to the death.

The division remained in the Admiralties until October 1944, with its units scattered over the islands providing security as bases were developed, mop-up patrols were conducted, and replacements were given a taste of on-the-job training. Major General Mudge took command of the division in August, and planning began for the Leyte landing.

Originally Mindanao in the southern Philippines was to be seized in mid-November and the Leyte landing was scheduled for December 20, but owing to weaker than expected Japanese air and naval activity it was decided to bypass Mindanao and assault Leyte on October 20. This was a dangerous

Near San José, Leyte, in October 1944, 1st Cavalry Division troopers wade a flooded antitank ditch to sweep through a shell-battered village. Note the jungle packs with attached M1910 entrenching tools. (US Army)

proposition; Leyte was in the heart of the Philippines surrounded by Japanese-held islands, open to reinforcement from Luzon, and there were no Allied airbases within range for close air support. Assigned to X Corps along with the 24th Inf Div, the 1st Cav departed the Admiralties on October 12 after conducting landing rehearsals. Three days before boarding the 82d Field Artillery Bn was given 105mm howitzers to replace its 75mm packs, deemed too light for jungle warfare. The division would fight in brigade combat teams of two cavalry regiments, each supported by a 75mm or 105mm battalion, an engineer troop, medical collecting company, attached surgical hospital, and other attachments as required.

LEYTE AND SAMAR

A-Day for the landings, on a 16-mile stretch of the island's upper east coast, was October 20, 1944. One of four assault divisions, the 1st Cav landed on Sixth Army's north flank near San José, with the 24th Inf Div to its left and XXIV Corps further to the south. Resistance was light, as the Japanese 16th Div's main defense line was well inland behind the coastal swamps, which proved troublesome. Some of the assault squadrons came ashore in amphibian tractors in the late morning, the troopers struggling through the chest-deep swamps to secure the Cataisan peninsula and Tacloban airfield, but by nightfall all objectives had been reached. The relentless rain and clinging mud would be secondary enemies throughout the campaign.

The next morning the 7th Cavalry moved north to fight its way into Tacloban, the island's capital – where they received a joyous welcome from Filipinos – but the Japanese were still dug in outside; 2/7 Cavalry took Hill 215 the next day, killing 335 defenders. The 1st Bde in the south of the division's zone pushed inland through difficult swamps. At this point the Japanese believed the main American effort to be in the south, but 1st Cav had the critical mission of securing Sixth Army's northern flank from any threat out of Leyte Valley, taking existing airstrips for improvement, and securing the narrow San Jacinto Strait between Leyte and the large island of Samar to the northeast. On October 22 the 8th Cavalry was released to the division, and the 1st Bde cleared the high ground around Tacloban. The divisional CP was established in the city, and soon confronted a serious problem in the form of 50,000 Filipinos needing food, clothing, shelter, and medical care. Ill-prepared for this situation, the Americans provided what they could and opened up Japanese warehouses.

For the rest of the month the 1st Cavalry and 24th Infantry divisions would battle for northern Leyte. On the 23rd, the 1st Bde went into corps reserve and 2d Bde commenced its drive up Highway 1 to the island's northern end. The 8th Cavalry was in the lead, and on October 24 crossed over to Samar to clear the area along the strait; at the same time the 1/7 Cav sailed north through the strait in landing craft and landed at Babatngon on Leyte's north coast. The rest of the regiment pushed north from Tacloban while the 12th Cavalry continued to clear the hills, and on October 25 all the initial objectives had been achieved for light casualties. The 1st Bde was employed to assist the advance of the 24th Inf Div, which was experiencing unexpected resistance as it fought its way over the road to Carigara Bay, and the rest of the 2d Bde moved onto Samar. The 1st Bde's missions including advancing north across the Leyte Valley; advancing west through the mountains to attack the enemy flank and rear in Ormoc Valley; breaking through the mountain passes into Ormoc Valley, and mopping up remaining resistance there. Rain continued to slow operations. The 1/7th conducted a series of waterborne movements along the north coast, advancing toward Carigara where the Japanese were delivering supplies. Guerrilla reports indicated the Japanese were preparing to make a stand at Carigara, and X Corps directed the 1st Cav to delay its attack until the 24th Inf Div was in position to support it. The 12th Cavalry remained in corps reserve, mopping up in the rear, while the 5th Cavalry secured the line-of-communications.

The attack on Carigara began on November 1 with an attack in squadron column: 1/7, 2/8, and 2/5 Cavalry. The Japanese had evacuated the town, and by November 3 they had abandoned the north end of the Leyte Valley. The 12th Cavalry reverted to division control and the division was assigned the mission of preventing any Japanese reinforcement landings in the area; while 10,000 Japanese had been destroyed to date, they had succeeded in landing 20,000 men at Ormoc Bay on Leyte's west coast. Stragglers were mopped up and encounters with Japanese groups increased. The cavalrymen excelled in patrolling, and combat patrols became the accepted means of

1st Cavalry Division Task Organization Leyte, October 1944

1st Cavalry Brigade Combat Team

HQ & HQ Tp, 1st Bde

5th Cav Regt (Special)

12th Cav Regt (Special)

Tp A, 8th Engineer Sqn

Co A, 44th Tank Bn

Co A, 85th Chemical Bn (4.2in mortar)

302d Recon Tp (–2 platoons)

1st Collecting Co, 1st Medical Sqn

19th MPS Hospital

section, 39th QM War Dog Plat

2d Cavalry Brigade Combat Team

HQ & HQ Tp, 2d Bde

7th Cav Regt (Special)

Tp C, 8th Engineer Sqn

Cos B & D, 44th Tank Bn

Co B, 85th Chemical Bn (4.2in mortar)

Co A, 826th Amphibious Tractor Bn

2d Collecting Co, 1st Medical Sqn

27th MPS Hospital

Division and Corps Reserve

8th Cav Regt (Special)

44th Tank Bn (–4 companies)

85th Chemical Bn (–4 companies)

Unit 2, 240th Chemical Composite Co

Co B, 632d Tank Destroyer Bn (M18)

3d & 4th Plats, 302d Recon Tp

The swamps of the Leyte Valley were as much a hindrance to the cavalrymen's advance as the enemy, and they would find the going no easier once they reached the forested hills. (US Army)

locating the enemy, overcoming moderate resistance, and securing lightly defended objectives. Enemy reinforcements were flowing north from Ormoc Bay as the Japanese attempted to halt the advance of the 1st Cav and 24th Inf divisions, but the capture of the bay would prevent their further reinforcement.

The 12th Cavalry attacked into the high ground on the left flank of the Leyte Valley on November 9. During the approach march a typhoon battered the island, but despite strong resistance in the hills, inaccurate maps, resupply problems in the difficult terrain, and insistent rain the 1st Cav pushed west, now with the 24th Inf Div on its north flank. The 112th Cavalry arrived on Leyte on November 14 and was attached to the division's 1st Bde two

F · DIGGING IN ON LOS NEGROS: 5th CAVALRY, FEBRUARY 1943

The reconnaissance-in-force landing on February 29, 1943 found the 5th Cavalry digging in on Momote airfield on Los Negros. The beachhead behind the perimeter was so small that the 75mm pack howitzers could not cover the ground in front of the perimeter, and the crews became riflemen. The .50cal AA machine guns were set up on the perimeter to help mow down the Japanese attacks. Troopers digging in on the 1,500-yard perimeter line found that the ground was concrete-hard coral, and no barbed wire or sandbags were available. However, the Japanese were forced to attack across the open airfield runway; their attacks on the first night

resulted in seven dead Americans and 15 wounded, but left 66 Japanese dead inside the perimeter alone.

The cavalrymen had been issued olive drab herringbone twill fatigues – good coloration for the jungle, but hot and slow-drying. The troopers were equipped with M1928 backpacks and other infantry web gear. A high percentage of Thompson .45cal M1 submachine guns were issued, which were not authorized on the equipment tables; the 1st Cav Div swore by the value of this close-ranged weapon's firepower in the jungle. They also used .30cal M1 carbines, but found they lacked the necessary penetration in the dense jungle, and the .30cal M1 rifle was preferred.

(Inset) 5th Cavalry Regiment

Cavalry troopers fight their way through a shattered village of nipa-palm huts; Japanese snipers and grenade-throwers could be hidden anywhere in the wreckage. The fixed bayonets were used to probe through the debris. (US Army)

days later; this gave the division ten squadrons. While its infantry strength was still less than that of a standard infantry division, the smaller squadrons could maneuver more easily in the forested hills than the bigger infantry battalions. The first 112th elements went into the line on November 18 when 1/112th relieved 1/7th.

By November 20 resistance was again strengthening; increasingly large strongpoints were encountered and the Japanese hill positions were difficult to reduce. Unless an artillery barrage impacted directly on a ridge crest position it either landed below the ridge top or went over to land in the valley, or even struck the next hill. The Japanese would pull down the reverse slope until the barrage had been adjusted onto their position, then would immediately reoccupy the position as the cavalrymen struggled up the forward slope through slippery mud, meeting them with a withering fire. The troopers' 60mm, 81mm, and 4.2in mortars proved especially valuable, as they could be moved up close to the fighting and could more easily engage reverse slope positions. The Japanese cut fields of fire low in the vegetation and the climbing troops did not realize that they were within them until too late; the defenders would roll grenades down the slopes while the cavalrymen throwing their grenades uphill were hampered by vegetation. Multiple troops and parts of troops would have to attack positions from different directions to overcome them, and while the cavalrymen attacked the Japanese attempted to infiltrate in other sectors, requiring constant combat patrols to counter these efforts. (While all this was underway the 8th Cavalry continued to patrol Samar, and with the support of the 99th Field Artillery they finally cleared the central portion of the island.)

Getting supplies to the front was a continuing problem. Trucks carried supplies and ammunition 30 miles from the beachhead up the Leyte Valley, where they had to be transferred to amtracs of the 826th Amphibious Tractor Bn to haul them across a few miles of flooded rice paddies. Then they were transferred to cargo trailers pulled by caterpillar tractors, sometimes in tandem, for the crawl up into the hills. Native porters, paid by the Army and protected by guerrillas, carried rations and supplies to the front in relays, a task sometimes requiring four days. There was no continuous US front line, the units being scattered widely in the rugged terrain with many gaps. The Japanese managed to infiltrate the supply routes and even establish positions astride them; this disrupted resupply, so units were constantly low on rations and ammunition, and the 12th Cavalry expended much effort clearing the routes. By the beginning of December the cavalrymen had killed more than 2,000 enemy and taken 125 prisoners; their own losses were 133 dead, 490 wounded, and seven missing.

The 1/112th attempted to slip behind Japanese lines to cut their supply route, and had some success. On December 14 the 7th Cavalry managed to destroy a particularly resilient strongpoint that had held out for two weeks, and Troop G was awarded the Presidential Unit Citation for this action. From the next day the 5th Cavalry established a screen and trail blocks while the 7th, 12th, and 112th consolidated their gains and continued their advance southwards into the foothills at the north end of the Ormoc Valley. (On Samar, meanwhile, the 8th Cavalry liberated the capital of Catbalogan on the 20th, and what little organized resistance remained withdrew to the north end of the island.) That same day the 12th Cavalry renewed its push down the highway through the Ormoc Valley toward Canang; now out of the hills, it had room to maneuver, while the advances of the 7th and 112th Cavalry were still slowed by broken ground. On December 23 the 12th, 5th, and 7th Cavalry turned west to clear the Ormoc peninsula, with the 77th Inf Div to their north and the 32d to the south. This was mainly a mop-up of scattered, disorganized units and stragglers trying to reach the west coast in hope of rescue, and the terrain of ridges and swamps was more of a hindrance than the enemy. In the early hours 200–300 Japanese who launched a banzai charge against a 12th Cavalry troop were wiped out, but the Japanese were not finished yet; patrols were still being ambushed, and there were close calls when small units were surrounded. Although organized resistance was declared destroyed on December 25 fighting continued, with the 5th, 7th, and 12th Cavalry still hunting holdouts, the 112th mopping up in the rear,

Troopers of 1st Sqn, 7th Cavalry advance through a village supported by M4 Shermans of the division's attached 44th Tank Battalion. (US Army)

Leyte's mud was not only a hindrance to foot troops, but hampered and endangered the logistics effort. The ceaseless rains saturated the low ground, turning it into bottomless muck, and in some areas even full-tracked vehicles could not negotiate the sea of mud. (US Army)

and the 8th on Samar chasing stragglers. Additional casualties were suffered, but the regiments began moving to assembly areas, and apart from the 8th Cavalry most were back in the Leyte Valley by January 2, 1945.

X and XXIV Corps and their seven divisions were transferred to Eighth Army control on December 26. US casualties had been light for a force of this size, but the terrain and weather had been brutal. Counting the reinforcements sent from Luzon, the Japanese had lost over four divisions, which helped reduce the forces available for the defense of Luzon. In all the 1st Cavalry Division lost 241 dead, two missing, and 856 wounded, while killing over 6,000 Japanese; the 112th Cavalry lost only 32 dead and 127 wounded. The division had become very proficient in patrolling and hill fighting. The degree of teamwork developed between the cavalry squadrons and supporting artillery was superior, and would serve the division well during the coming battles on Luzon.

G **FIREFIGHT ON LEYTE:**
12th CAVALRY, NOVEMBER 1944

There were countless examples of valor in the jungled, rain-drenched hills of Leyte, and one of one of these brief but violent actions occurred on November 7, 1944. Sergeant Curtis L. Spoon was leading his understrength rifle squad of Troop B, 12th Cavalry on a combat patrol when they received heavy rifle fire from a hillside hut. Understanding the value of prisoners, Sgt Spoon directed his squad's fire into the hut while he advanced alone, charged into the position, killed two Japanese and took three prisoners.

The eight-man cavalry rifle squad was normally led by a corporal, sometimes a sergeant, and included six riflemen and an automatic rifleman with a .30cal M1918A2 BAR. Squad leaders usually had a .45cal M1 Thompson SMG; some preferred the .30cal M1 Garand rifle and another squad member carried the Tommy-gun. The Thompson, while heavy, was well liked for the close combat amid jungle-clad hills; it proved less valuable in the open Ormoc Valley owing to longer combat ranges, but its value was again realized in the streets of Manila. The BAR was valuable in both the hills and the valley, but it was heavy and cumbersome, and was also difficult to keep operational in the wet, muddy, tropical environment. The Thompsons and BARs were invaluable to the rifle platoon as they were the only automatic weapons available other than a mere two .30cal M1919A4 Browning LMGs in the machine gun section of the troop weapons platoon. **(Inset)** 12th Cavalry Regiment

LUZON

The completion of the Leyte campaign and the assembly of the 1st Cav Div in the first days of 1945 brought no respite for the battle-worn cavalrymen after their ten weeks of intense combat under brutal conditions. Preparations began immediately for movement to the main objective of the Philippines liberation campaign – the great northern island of Luzon, occupied by Gen Yamashita's 250,000-strong Fourteenth Area Army. Only a handful of replacements were received, and worn and lost equipment was not replaced; while the men were issued fresh clothes and fed hot meals, many vehicles were on the verge of breakdown after hard use with little maintenance. A few officer reassignments were made; the regiments were at about half strength, and many enlisted men were field-promoted to fill vacant lieutenant slots. The only favorable factor was that the division did not have to absorb and try to train green replacements; they would go back into battle in the same proficient combat teams they had perfected over the past two months. Nevertheless, no other US division in the Pacific Theater was ever committed to a major invasion so grossly understrength. At least it would not be conducting an assault landing, but was part of a follow-on force.

The Sixth Army landed unopposed, except for air attacks, on the morning of January 9, 1945 – S-Day – in the southern end of Lingayen Gulf on the upper west coast of Luzon. The island was too large for a coastline defense with the available assets, and most Japanese forces were withdrawing north into the rugged central mountains, leaving only small units to conduct delaying actions as Sixth Army pushed southwards down the Agno/Pampanga river valley (over the same ground where the 26th Cavalry had fought three years earlier). Embarking on January 25 for the short voyage from Leyte to Luzon, the 1st Cav Div were subjected to air attacks including *kamikaze* raids, but the clean bunks, showers, and hot shipboard food were a welcome boost to morale. The 112th Cavalry remained attached to the division and were accepted as an integral component, as was the 44th Tank Battalion.

On January 27 the 1st Cav landed at Mabilao, and after a 30-mile march to Guimba the division was attached to XIV Corps alongside the 40th and 37th Infantry Divisions. On January 31 Gen MacArthur visited the division

On Luzon the 1st Cavalry Brigade's "flying column" covered over 100 heavily contested miles in 66 hours to charge into Manila, to liberate University Santo Tomas and its civilian internees as well as other key sites. Every available vehicle was used to mount the column's troops. (US Army)

and gave MajGen Mudge a set of simple instructions: "Go to Manila. Go around the Nips, bounce off the Nips, but go to Manila. Free the internees at Santo Thomas. Take Malacañang Palace and the Legislative Building." Mudge assigned the mission to the 1st Bde, and BrigGen Chase organized three "serials" using all available vehicles, with troopers riding on tanks; they were to make a lightning-fast cavalry-style strike into the heart of Manila, 100 miles to the south.

On the same day the 11th Airborne Division landed south of Manila. Three divisions – 37th Inf, 1st Cav, and 11th Abn – were closing in on the capital from different directions, and it would soon become a race to see who would enter the city first.

Traveling light and with only four days' rations and ammunition, the three serials departed in the first hour of February 1, moving on three different roads toward Cabanatuan 20 miles to the southeast; the rest of 1st Bde followed with the 7th and 12th Cavalry. The rapid advance allowed some bridges to be captured intact, but a Japanese demolition truck intending to blow one bridge was detonated by a US bazookaman, creating a massive road crater that took engineers a day to fill. On reaching Cabanatuan it was discovered that a nearby prison camp had already been liberated and the prisoners evacuated by a daring Ranger raid the day before.

That evening BrigGen Chase was given direct command of the three serials as the now combined flying column continued its advance to Manila. The road was clear; a destroyed bridge forced a detour, but the column plunged on, under continuous air cover provided by Marine Aircraft Groups 23 and 32. At times destroyed bridges and roadblocks halted the advance; all bridges over the Angat River had been wrecked, but the cavalrymen discovered a ford, which required engineer squadron assistance. The aim was to avoid decisive engagements and thrust into Manila to rescue the 3,700 US, British, Australian, Canadian, Dutch, and other nationality internees at Santo Thomas University. At Baliuag the force split into two columns, and Piper Cub spotter planes of the 82d Field Artillery Bn guided the way through the

1st Cav Bde Manila flying column

1st Serial

2d Sqn, 5th Cavalry Regt (Special)

Recon Platoon, HQ Troop, 5th Cav Regt

Antitank Plat, HQ Tp, 5th Cav Regt

Medical Detachment, 5th Cav Regt

Co A, 44th Tank Bn

Bty A, 82d Field Arty Bn

3d Plat, Tp A, 8th Engineer Sqn

1st Plat, Tp A, 1st Medical Sqn

2d Serial

2d Sqn, 8th Cav Regt (Special)

Recon Plat, HQ Troop, 8th Cav Regt

AT Plat, HQ Tp, 8th Cav Regt

.50cal MG Section, Weapons Tp, 8th Cav Regt

Maintenance Sect, HQ Tp, 8th Cav Regt

Co B, 44th Tank Bn

Bty B, 61st Field Arty Bn

1st Plat, Tp C, 8th Engineer Sqn

1st Plat, Tp B, 1st Medical Sqn

3d Serial

44th Tank Bn (–Cos A & B)

302d Recon Tp (Mechanized)

The 44th Tank Bn was instrumental to the success of the "flying column", providing fire support and mobility with troopers riding on the Sherman tanks. (US Army)

city's outskirts. The troopers barreled across the city limits at 1835hrs on February 3, making them the first US force to enter Manila; at 2050hrs, guided by guerrillas, they reached the university. They had covered 100 miles, overcoming rearguard actions and destroyed bridges, in 66 hours.

After a brief skirmish 8th Cavalry troops reached Santo Thomas with five tanks. The guards gathered 200 internees in a building and threatened to kill them, but the Americans negotiated their release in return for promising the guards safe passage to a point near Malacañang the next day. (The Japanese were escorted there with their personal weapons only; unbeknownst to them the town had been occupied by the Americans, and the surviving guards soon found themselves back at the university as prisoners.) The internees were in a pitiable condition; the troopers gave up what little food they had until the Catholic bishop was able to collect more, and XIV Corps sent in a field hospital to care for the liberated internees. Malacañang Palace (the Philippine White House) was secured by F/8 Cav on February 3, but the Japanese were able to blow the Pasig River bridges and the flying column was unable to reach the Legislative Building. It would not be taken for another month.

MANILA

Over the next couple of days more 1st Cav troops flowed into Manila and spread out to secure key positions. One of these was the Novaliches dam, the city's main source of water, which was one of many facilities that the Japanese had rigged for demolition. 1/5 Cav struggled to keep open the lines to the rear as supply convoys ran a gauntlet of ambushes to support the troops fighting inside the city.

On February 7, Gen MacArthur entered the city and congratulated the flying column troops on their bold effort; BrigGen Chase of the 1st Bde was promoted to take command of 38th Inf Div, and recommended Col Harry Stadler of the 12th Cavalry to take over. To date the 1st Cav had lost only 36 dead, four missing, and 141 wounded while killing 1,600 Japanese and capturing 51.

An 8th Cavalry machine-gun squad armed with a .30cal M1919A2 sets up to defend the university after reaching it on February 3, 1945. (1st Cavalry Division Museum)

On the 8th, the 27th Inf Div took over responsibly for clearing the northern portion of Manila and the 1st Cav the southern, south of the Pasig River, which the engineers bridged with pontoons. (The bridge was knocked out by Japanese artillery twice, but was always made operational within a short time.) On February 12 the 12th Cavalry was relieved of its line-of-communications security duties by the 112th, joining the rest of the division in the bitter city fighting and relieving the 8th Cavalry. That same day the 5th Cavalry secured Nielson Field on the southeast side of the city, reached Manila Bay, and linked up with the 11th Abn Div attacking from the southeast; the city was now encircled and the Japanese were trapped. 1/5 Cav attacked toward Ft William McKinley also on the southeast side of the city.

BrigGen William Chase, commanding 1st Cavalry Bde, at University Santo Thomas; his escorts are armed with M1928A1 Thompson SMGs. General Chase provided the model for the fictional "Sam Damon" in the 1968 novel, *Once an Eagle*. (1st Cavalry Division Museum)

Over 20,000 Japanese were resolutely dug in as the US forces gradually compressed their perimeter. Fighting a stubborn, well dug-in enemy in a large modern city was an entirely new experience for the cavalrymen. Progress was slow, but the remaining defenders were squeezed into the Intramuros, the fortress-like former Spanish seat of government. To better coordinate the encirclement, on February 16 the division's 1st Bde was placed under the control of 37th Inf Div; that same day the 112th Cavalry threw back a determined 500-man, artillery-supported attack, possibly an attempted breakout. Pfc William J. Grabiarz of F/5 Cav earned the Medal of Honor on February 23 as he ran to recover his troop CO lying wounded in the open; wounded himself, he was unable to drag the officer to cover, but shielded him with his body until riddled by the Japanese as a tank maneuvered in to rescue the captain.

The fighting continued for almost two more hellish weeks as the troops shot, blasted, and burned their way through defended buildings. Much of Manila was destroyed even though only point-blank artillery fire was employed and air strikes were restricted. During this time the 2d Cav Bde had held high ground east of the city to prevent reinforcements from infiltrating. On March 3 the last resistance crumbled; XIV Corps had suffered 6,500 causalities and up to 100,000 Filipinos had died in the fighting. The Japanese lost at least 16,000 men in and around the city.

SOUTHERN LUZON

In the meantime XIV Corps began an offensive on February 20 to clear southern Luzon. XI Corps took over on March 14, taking charge of the in-place divisions – 11th Abn and 6th, 38th and 43d Inf Divs – and the 1st Cav also joined the fight. On February 20 the 2d Bde was relieved by elements of the 6th Inf Div and directed to move east to attack the Shimbu Line; the 112th Cavalry was attached to the 6th Div, and would remain so until late March. First-rate Japanese troops waited to fight for the rugged hills of the Picol peninsula jutting 200 miles to the southeast; the 2d Bde crossed the Maraquina River unopposed and took up positions to commence the assault.

By February 25 the 7th and 8th Cavalry were approaching the Antipolo area where the Japanese were dug in on a series of ridges honeycombed with

Cavalrymen advance up a dust-shrouded street during the month-long battle for Manila. The troopers had to make a rapid adaptation to fighting in a large modern city after long months of combat amid jungles, swamps, and hills. (1st Cavalry Division Museum)

caves and tunnels. They defended these stubbornly, and divisional engineers and regimental pioneer and demolition platoons, along with direct artillery fire and air strikes, were needed to blast them out of their fortifications. At the end of February BrigGen Hugh F.T. Hoffman of 2d Bde took over command of the division from the seriously wounded MajGen Mudge, and the 8th Cavalry's Col William J. Bradley took over the brigade. On March 6 the 1st Bde, after a short rest from the Manila battle, moved in on the north side of the 2d Bde. In one horrible incident flamethrower operators flamed a cave and over 100 burning Japanese charged out firing their weapons to be cut down by machine guns; 147 dead were counted outside the cave alone. The 43d Inf Div relieved the 1st Cav on March 12; in the 20 days since February 21, men of the division had been awarded 92 Silver Stars and a Distinguished Service Cross.

The division was given a well-earned rest south of Manila until sent back into action again on March 23, but no replacements were received except for a few recovered casualties. Through March and into April 1945 a two-pronged attack cleared the area south of Laguna de Bay and the east shore of Lake Teal. During this period the division operated in two brigade columns, usually with a third squadron attached to one of its regiments while the "one-squadron" regiment mopped up. From April 23 to May 3 the 8th Cavalry and 2/7 Cav were attached to the 11th Airborne Division. Southeast of Laguna de Bay was a large mass of hills which it took the 12th Cavalry from May 6 to 26 to clear. The 2d Bde began pushing down the Picol peninsula and cleared the Mt Malepunyo area, the 5th Cavalry moving south while the 12th spread out across the peninsula to catch stragglers and secure the line-of-communications. Squadron- and troop-sized operations were the rule; 2/5 Cav made their way down the peninsula along with the 158th RCT, and Troop B, 1/5 Cav and an engineer troop conducted an unopposed amphibious landing at Pasacao on the night of April 26/27 to link up with the advance. On May 1 the 5th Cavalry was attached to the 158th RCT to complete the drive to destroy the estimated 3,000 Japanese in the Mt Isarog area, while the 1st Bde (less 5th Cavalry) was pulled back to clear other areas. The 5th Cavalry was released by the 158th in early June, when operations in the south were drawing down, though a great deal of mopping up was still required throughout the peninsula. Southern Luzon was declared secure on May 31, but small actions and clean-up operations continued, and it was not until the end of June that all of Luzon was declared secure.

In the process of killing over 14,000 Japanese and taking 1,199 prisoners on Luzon, the 1st Cav Div lost 680 dead, three missing, and 2,334 wounded. The 112th RCT began the Luzon operation with 130 officers and 2,191 enlisted out of an authorized strength of 153 and 2,478, respectively; it ended the campaign with 125 and 2,087. The RCT received almost 750 replacements while suffering over 200 combat casualties, but they also replaced the many non-combat casualties.

A 5th Cavalry gunner covers a street against snipers with his .30cal M1917A1 water-cooled heavy machine gun. Eight of these reliable and highly accurate support weapons were assigned to squadron weapons troops. (1st Cavalry Division Museum)

OCCUPATION OF JAPAN

The division gradually assembled at Lucena in June, and while it rested it received more replacements than ever before, undergoing a major reorganization in July. It was planned that on November 1, 1945 the division and 112th Cavalry would take part in the invasion of Kyushu, the southernmost of the Home Islands, under XI Corps. The five cavalry regiments were assigned the table of organization and equipment of standard infantry regiments, except for still having only two squadrons and no antitank troop. Squadron and troop designations were retained. The 947th Field Artillery Bn (155mm Howitzer) had been assigned in January; this provided a 105mm

In southern Luzon the division fought on the 200-mile long Picol peninsula. Units operating near the coasts were often resupplied by Engineer Special Brigade landing craft such as the LCM(3) – Landing Craft, Mechanized. (1st Cavalry Division Museum)

HONOR·AND·COURAGE·

8th Cavalry troopers with one of the 3,700 liberated civilian internees; note the jungle-worn fatigues and caps that the troopers have been wearing since Leyte and Samar. The internees did not at first recognize the cavalrymen as Americans, having never before seen the green fatigues and M1 carbines. (US Army)

battalion for each cavalry regiment and a divisional general support battalion. This gave the division roughly the same capabilities as other infantry divisions, and with the attachment of the 112th it had ten infantry battalions. Colonel Philip L. Hooper took command of the 112th in July 1945.

On August 1, MajGen Chase returned from the 38th Inf Div and assumed command of the 1st Cav, BrigGen Hoffman reverting to command of the 2d Bde. On August 13 a warning order was issued alerting the division to prepare for movement to Japan in event of a breakdown in the government after the detonation of the atomic bombs, and it was assigned to the Eighth Army. Japan announced its intention to capitulate on August 14; the surrender was scheduled for August 31, but a typhoon delayed the Third Fleet and the

H MANILA STREET FIGHT: 8th CAVALRY, FEBRUARY 1945

The "flying column's" 2d Sqn, 8th Cavalry tore into Manila city on February 3, 1945, aiming to liberate civilian internees and secure key facilities; they reached St Thomas University with five M4 Sherman medium tanks from Co B, 44th Tank Battalion. Machine guns were found at three echelons in the cavalry regiment. The rifle troop's weapons platoon possessed a section of two .30cal M1919A4 light machine guns, which could be attached one to each forward rifle platoon, or the section attached to a platoon, or the section retained under troop control. The 1st Cavalry Division was unique in that it retained the technically obsolete M1919A2 cavalry machine gun **(foreground)** in some units, with a barrel 5.37in shorter than the 24in of the M1919A4. The squadron weapons troop had two platoons each with four .30cal M1917A1 water-cooled heavy machine guns (not pictured) plus a platoon of six 81mm

M1 mortars. The regimental weapons troop was organized the same, but substituted .50cal M2 HMGs for the M1917A1s; two-gun sections were usually attached directly to rifle troops or squadron weapons troops **(background)**. No other infantry unit possessed ".50cals" with dedicated crews; in most units they were mounted on vehicles for air defense. The cavalry employed weapons-troop .50cals for supporting fires to engage longer-ranged targets, fortified buildings, and vehicles, and to chop though heavy jungle vegetation. While the barrel was relatively easy to remove, this was not done to ease the burden when carried; two men carried the 85lb gun complete with the barrel (it would have taken a couple of minutes to screw the barrel back in and set the headspace.) Another man carried the 44lb M3 tripod and the rest of the section carried 100-round ammunition cans.

(Inset) 8th Cavalry Regiment

Signal troops lay field telephone wire on Luzon using DR-4 reels, holding 4 miles of wire, on an RL-21 reel unit stand. The constantly advancing units moved so rapidly at times that there was no time to recover wire, and new wire was simply laid. (1st Cavalry Division Museum)

ceremony would take place on September 2. The 1st Cav Div with the 112th Cavalry departed Manila on August 25 and was off the coast of Japan on the morning of September 2 for the historic event. Prepared for resistance of any form, the division landed at 1100hrs at the Yokohama docks (the large city and naval base across the bay from Tokyo). While the troops were apprehensive, the division's leadership was not overly concerned; an advance party had arrived five days earlier by air and the chief of staff had gone ashore half an hour earlier and gave the all clear. The division secured the city and five airfields on its outskirts. On September 8 the 1st Cav was the first US force to enter Tokyo (a reconnaissance party had already entered on the 5th.)

The Japanese were completely cooperative and the occupation went smoothly. The division's mission was to secure critical facilities and conduct patrols to locate military installations and depots, and to locate, inventory and remove all war materials for disposal. Many unusual assignments were undertaken, including seizing financial records from all banks for investigation and seizing precious metals. The division was eventually responsible for an area of 5,000 square miles around Tokyo and a population of 20 million. The 112th disarmed 70 Japanese combat units and bases. The artillery battalions were re-roled as infantry and in effect were dismounted themselves. The 531st and 720th Military Police Bns were attached to the division during this period. As other occupation units were inactivated or returned to the States, the 1st Cav received thousands of green troops from these units who had served only a short time overseas. It was not long before all the combat veterans had returned home.

After the dash to Manila and the subsequent battle for the city the 1st Cav's campaign was far from over; they still faced weeks of fighting in the paddies and jungled hills of southern Luzon. (1st Cavalry Division Museum)

The 1st Cavalry Division had performed extraordinarily well in its three campaigns. It had met the challenges of converting from cavalry to infantry, and had usually succeeded in all its mission requirements even though it was much below the strength of its infantry counterparts. Divisional units received ten Presidential Unit Citations, and the division was awarded the Philippine Presidential Unit Citation.

* * *

The 112th Cavalry was inactivated at Tateyama, Japan on January 17, 1946. It was reassigned, on paper, to the Texas National Guard on July 2, 1946, but no elements were raised yet. The 12th Cavalry Regiment was inactivated on March 25, 1949 in Otawa, Japan. The 5th, 7th, and 8th Cavalry and all elements of the division were reorganized and redesignated the same as any other infantry division. At the same time the regiments' squadrons and troops were redesignated battalions and companies, and they received 3d Battalions. With no need for the 1st and 2d Cavalry Bdes, these echelons were inactivated on March 2, 1949.

The 1st Cavalry Division remained in Japan until deployed to Korea from 1950–51, and then back to Japan. In 1957 the division was reduced to zero strength and the 24th Infantry Division in Korea was reflagged as the 1st Cavalry.[6]

The division remained there until 1965, when it exchanged colors with the 2d Infantry Division at Ft Benning, Georgia, where the existing 2d Infantry and 11th Air Assault Divisions were combined into the new 1st Cavalry Division (Airmobile). The cavalrymen were again mounted, but this time in helicopters. The division fought in Vietnam from 1965 to 1971, part of it remaining until 1972. Stationed at Ft Hood, Texas, it was reorganized as an experimental Triple Capability (TRICAP) division with mechanized, tank, and airmobile battalions, and attack helicopter squadrons. The concept proved unworkable, and in 1975 it was converted to an armored division with tank and mechanized battalions. It fought in the 1990–91 Gulf War, and the division or elements kept the peace in Kuwait in 1994–97 and in Bosnia in 1995–99. Elements fought in the 2003 Iraq War, with the

September 1945: 112th Cavalry troopers unload from a Japanese Nissan 180 1/2-ton cargo truck in Yokohama, Japan. The advance party of the occupation force had ordered the Japanese armed forces to provide specified numbers of operational trucks and sedans with drivers, but the US had to provide the fuel since the Japanese had exhausted their own stocks. (Texas Military Forces Museum)

entire division deploying there from 2004–05 and 2006–07. Through all this the 5th, 7th, 8th, and 12th (reactivated in 1957) Cavalry lineages have designated the division's maneuver battalions, be they airmobile infantry (three for a time were also airborne), mechanized infantry, tank, armored cavalry, or combined arms (mechanized infantry and tank).

The 112th Cavalry was reactivated as the 112th Armor in 1947 as the parent unit for Texas National Guard tank battalions in the 49th Armored Division and various separate brigades. The 124th Cavalry was reactivated in 1959 to provide the parent unit for Texas NG armored cavalry/reconnaissance squadrons and troops in the 36th Infantry and 49th Armored Divisions as well as separate brigades. Elements of both regiments have served in Iraq and continue to do so.

A 1st Cavalry Division trooper supervises Japanese workers shoveling up gold coins. The division oversaw the confiscation of tons of precious metals in the Tokyo area. (US Army

SELECT BIBLIOGRAPHY

Banks, Herbert C., *1st Cavalry Division: A Spur Ride Through the 20th Century "From Horses to the Digital Battlefield"* (Nashville, TN; Turner Publishing, 2003)

Cannon, M. Hamlin, *United States Army in World War II: Leyte: The Return to the Philippines* (Washington, DC; Center for Military History, 1987)

Chase, William C., *Front Line General: The Commands of William C. Chase* (Houston, TX; Pacesetter Press, 1975) (re 1st Cav Bde, 5th & 12th Cavalry)

Dera, Edward J., *Defending the Driniumor: Covering Force Operations in New Guinea, 1944*, Leavenworth Papers No. 9 (Ft Leavenworth; Combat Studies Institute, 1984) (re 112th Cavalry)

Essen, Emmett M., *Shavetails and Bell Sharps: The History of the US Army Mule* (Lincoln, NE; University of Nebraska Press, 2000)

Greenfield, Kent R., Robert R. Palmer & Bell I. Wiley, *United States Army in World War II: The Fall of the Philippines* (Washington, DC; 1947) (re 26th Cavalry)

Johnson, Glenn T., *We Ain't no Heroes: The 112th Cavalry in World War II* (Denton, TX; History Without Borders, 2005)

Miller, John Jr., *United States Army in World War II: Cartwheel: The Reduction of Rabaul* (Washington, DC; Center for Military History, 1959) (re 1st Cav Div, 112th Cavalry)

Powell, James S., *Learning Under Fire: A Combat Unit in the Southwest Pacific* (College Station; Texas A&M University, 2006) (re 112th Cavalry. Dissertation available at: http://txspace.tamu.edu/bitstream/handle/1969

6 Rumors exist that the 1st Cav Div was "banned" from retuning to the States for losing its colors during the Korean War. The myth is based on the Nov 1950 Unsan engagement when the 8th Cavalry was pushed back by overwhelming Chinese forces – no colors were lost. The stationing of units is based on military need and the reflagging of divisions is determined by a point system.

A major inspects a corporal's M1 rifle. The corporal displays the 27th Infantry Division patch on his right shoulder, indicating that he had previously seen combat in that formation. He is evidently a "low point" man transferred into the 1st Cav from the 27th when the latter returned to the States. The large size of the 1st Cav's "saddle blanket" divisional patch can be seen here on the major's left shoulder; note the reversed presentation on the right side of the soldier's helmet liner. (1st Cavalry Division Museum)

.1/4237/etd-tamu-2006B-HIST-Powell-Copyright.pdf?sequence=1)

Randolph, John H., *Marsmen in Burma* (Houston, TX: Gulf Publishing, 1946–1990 r/p available) (re 124th Cavalry)

Romanus, Charles F., & Riley Sunderland, *United States Army in World War II: China-Burma-India Theater: Time Runs Out in CBI* (Washington, DC; Center for Military History, 1959) (re 124th Cavalry)

Rottman, Gordon L., *World War II Pacific Island Guide: A Geo-Military Study* (Westport, CT; Greenwood Press, 2002)

Smith, Robert R., *United States Army in World War II: Triumph in the Philippines* (Washington, DC; Center for Military History, 1963) (re 1st Cav Div, 112th Cavalry)

Stubs, Mary L., & Stanley R. Connor, *Army Lineage Series: Armor-Cavalry, Part I* (Washington, DC; Center for Military History, 1969)

Whitman, John W., *Bataan: Our Last Ditch* (New York; Hippocrene Books, 1990) (re 26th Cavalry)

Wright, Bertram R., *The 1st Cavalry Division in World War II* (Tokyo; Toppan Printing, 1947)

WEBSITES

1st Cavalry Division Association website: http://www.1cda.org/

The Society of the Military Horse, an online organization, promotes the study of cavalry: http://www.militaryhorse.org/

US Cavalry Association website: http://www.uscavalry.org/

INDEX

References to illustrations are shown in bold.
Plates are shown with page locators in brackets.